cook & enjoy

Chocolate

cook & enjoy

Chocolate

Delicious recipes for the everyday cook

This edition published by Parragon Books Ltd in 2016

LOVE FOOD is an imprint of Parragon Books Ltd

Parragon Books Ltd
Chartist House
15–17 Trim Street
Bath BA1 1HA, UK
www.parragon.com/lovefood

ISBN 978-1-4748-4400-0

Printed in China

Cover photography by Henry Sparrow
Cover home economy by Kirsten Fowle
Introduction by Linda Doeser

Notes for the Reader
This book uses both metric and imperial measurements. Follow the same units of measurement throughout; do not mix metric and imperial. All spoon measurements are level: teaspoons are assumed to be 5 ml, and tablespoons are assumed to be 15 ml. Unless otherwise stated, milk is assumed to be full fat, eggs and individual vegetables are medium, pepper is freshly ground black pepper and salt is table salt. Unless otherwise stated, all root vegetables should be peeled prior to using.

The times given are an approximate guide only. Preparation times differ according to the techniques used by different people and the cooking times may also vary from those given.

Cover image shows the Chocolate Ganache Cake on page 16, the ganache styled without the teardrops.

contents

Introduction

For many people, chocolate is right at the top of their list of favourite foodstuffs. Its sweet richness combined with its literally melt-in-the-mouth texture always make it a special treat. We give chocolates as birthday and anniversary gifts, make chocolate cakes for celebrations, impress our dinner guests with lavish chocolate desserts, boost our flagging energy in the mid-morning with a chocolate cookie or gooey muffin and soothe our souls at bedtime with a steaming mug of hot chocolate.

TYPES OF CHOCOLATE

Chocolate is made up of a mixture of cocoa and sugar, although other ingredients, such as milk, honey and ginger, may also be added. There are many different types of cocoa beans – the seeds of the cacao tree – ranging in colour from almost black to light brown and in flavour from mild to bitter. Whether they are ordinary or fine, the beans undergo a lengthy process of cleaning, roasting, cracking and grinding to produce chocolate liquor, which may then be transformed into cocoa butter for making chocolate or into cocoa powder.

The proportion of cocoa liquor to sugar determines the type of chocolate – the higher the ratio, the darker and more bitter the final result. The quality and type of the beans and the percentage of cocoa butter, as well as the care and expertise expended in its preparation, determine the quality of the chocolate. Price is often an indication of quality but you can also tell by the chocolate's appearance, texture and taste. Good quality chocolate is brown in colour, shiny, with no lumps, air holes or specks, and it should snap cleanly when broken.

It should melt on the tongue, releasing a rich chocolate flavour rather than the taste of cocoa, and the 'mouth feel' should be neither sticky nor greasy.

PLAIN CHOCOLATE is dark, lightly sweetened and should contain at least 50 per cent cocoa solids (check the label).

DARK CHOCOLATE is similar to plain chocolate, but more bitter with a very rich flavour.

MILK CHOCOLATE is made with the addition of milk solids and is lighter in colour, sweeter and milder in flavour than plain or dark chocolate.

WHITE CHOCOLATE is made from sweetened cocoa butter and, strictly speaking, is not chocolate at all. Technically, it is white confectionery coating, but most people call it white chocolate. You should use it only in recipes that specify white chocolate as it cannot be substituted for plain, dark or milk chocolate.

CHOCOLATE COUVERTURE is the name given to very high quality plain or dark chocolate with a high cocoa butter content. Milk and white chocolate couverture is also available. Couverture is widely used in the confectionery industry and by professional chefs for baking and making chocolate icings, sauces and mousses. However, it is quite tricky to handle and is not essential for most home baking.

COCOA POWDER, used for flavouring drinks, is unsweetened and has a strong flavour. It is widely used in baking.

DRINKING CHOCOLATE is a mixture of cocoa powder and sugar. It is mild in flavour, sweet and is best reserved for making drinks. As a general rule, drinking chocolate is not suitable for baking and cannot be used as a substitute for cocoa powder in recipes.

Top tips for cooking with chocolate

Chocolate is best stored in a cool place rather than the refrigerator, where it can become tainted with the smell of other foods and acquire a bloom on the surface. This is not harmful but does spoil the appearance of the chocolate.

Never melt chocolate on its own in a saucepan over direct heat as it scorches easily. However, it can be melted over a very low heat if it is combined with other ingredients such as butter, cream, milk or coffee. Stir occasionally and remove from the heat as soon as the chocolate has melted and the mixture is smooth.

To melt chocolate on its own, break it into small pieces and put them into a heatproof bowl, set over a saucepan of gently simmering water, making sure that the base of the bowl does not touch the surface of the water. Heat gently, stirring occasionally, until the chocolate has melted and is smooth, then remove from the heat. If melting white chocolate, chill it first, then grate finely into the bowl before heating.

If steam gets into the chocolate when you are melting it over simmering water, it is likely to solidify or seize. Stirring in 1 teaspoon of vegetable fat or grapeseed oil for every 25 g/1 oz chocolate will rectify the problem. The chocolate can then be used for baking or making desserts but is not suitable for making decorations, such as curls or leaves. This method does not work on seized white chocolate.

To melt chocolate in the microwave, break it into small pieces and put them into a microwave-safe bowl. Don't cover the bowl. Heat on Medium for 30 seconds, then stir and check whether it has melted. Continue heating, stirring and checking at 10-second intervals until the chocolate is smooth. You cannot tell whether it has melted simply by looking as it will hold its shape even when melted. White chocolate should be chilled before melting, finely grated, then heated on Low and checked frequently in the same way.

To make chocolate curls, shave the edge of a firm chocolate bar with a vegetable peeler. For a more professional decoration spread a thin layer of melted chocolate on a marble slab or chilled baking sheet and leave until just set. Holding a metal spatula or palette knife at a low angle, scrape the chocolate into long curls or scrolls.

To make chocolate leaves, use firm, clean shiny leaves with short stems, such as rose leaves. Brush the shiny side of the leaves with melted chocolate using a small paintbrush and leave to set on a baking sheet lined with greaseproof paper in a cool place. When it has set, carefully pull off the leaves by holding the stems.

cakes

chocolate fudge cake

Serves 8

Difficulty: Medium

Prep: 40 mins, plus cooling
Cook: 1 hour–1 hour 10 minutes

INGREDIENTS

55 g/2 oz plain chocolate

2 tbsp milk

175 g/6 oz plain white flour

1 tbsp baking powder

175 g/6 oz unsalted butter,
  softened, plus extra
  for greasing

175 g/6 oz dark muscovado
  sugar

3 eggs, beaten

1 tsp vanilla extract

milk chocolate curls or
  grated chocolate, to
  decorate

FROSTING

100 g/3½ oz plain chocolate

55 g/2 oz unsalted butter,
  softened

175 g/6 oz icing sugar

1 tsp vanilla extract

1 tbsp milk

STEP 1. Preheat the oven to 180°C/350°F/Gas Mark 4. Grease a 23-cm/9-inch round cake tin and line with baking paper. Put the chocolate and milk into a small saucepan over a low heat and heat, without boiling, until melted. Remove from the heat. Sift the flour and baking powder into a mixing bowl and add the butter, muscovado sugar, eggs and vanilla extract. Beat well until smooth, then stir in the melted chocolate mixture.

STEP 2. Spoon the mixture into the prepared tin and smooth the top level. Bake in the preheated oven for 50–60 minutes until firm to the touch and just beginning to shrink away from the side of the tin. Leave to cool in the tin for 10 minutes, then turn out onto a wire rack and leave to cool completely. Carefully slice the cooled cake horizontally into two layers.

STEP 3. To make the frosting, put the chocolate and butter into a small saucepan over a low heat and heat until melted. Remove from the heat and stir in the icing sugar, vanilla extract and milk, then beat well until smooth. Sandwich the cake layers together with half the frosting, then spread the remainder on top of the cake, swirling with a palette knife. Decorate with chocolate curls.

chocolate ganache cake

Serves 10

Difficulty: Hard

Prep: 40 mins, plus cooling and 3 hours chilling
Cook: 45 mins

INGREDIENTS

175 g/6 oz butter, plus extra
  for greasing

175 g/6 oz caster sugar

4 eggs, beaten

250 g/9 oz self-raising flour

1 tbsp cocoa powder

50 g/1¾ oz plain chocolate,
  melted

200 g/7 oz chocolate-
  flavoured cake covering

GANACHE

450 ml/16 fl oz cream

375 g/13 oz plain chocolate,
  broken into pieces

STEP 1. Preheat the oven to 180°C/350°F/Gas Mark 4. Grease a 20-cm/8-inch springform cake tin and line with baking paper. Put the butter and sugar into a mixing bowl and cream together until light and fluffy. Gradually add the eggs, beating well after each addition. Sift together the flour and cocoa powder and fold into the mixture. Fold in the melted chocolate.

STEP 2. Pour into the prepared tin and smooth the top. Bake in the preheated oven for 40 minutes, or until springy to the touch. Leave to cool in the tin for 10 minutes, then turn out onto a wire rack and leave to cool completely. Carefully slice the cooled cake horizontally into two layers.

STEP 3. To make the ganache, put the cream into a saucepan and bring to the boil, stirring. Add the chocolate and stir until melted. Pour into a bowl, leave to cool, then chill for 2 hours, or until set and firm. Whisk until light and fluffy. Reserve one third of the ganache and use the remainder to sandwich the cake together and spread over the top and sides of the cake.

STEP 4. Melt the cake covering and spread it over a large sheet of baking paper. Leave to cool until just set. Cut into strips a little wider than the height of the cake. Place the strips around the edge of the cake, overlapping them slightly. Pipe the reserved ganache in tear drops to cover the top of the cake. Leave to chill for 1 hour.

chocolate cake with syrup

Serves 12

Difficulty: Medium

Prep: 30 mins, plus cooling
Cook: 50 mins

INGREDIENTS

225 g/8 oz plain chocolate,
  broken into pieces

115 g/4 oz butter, plus extra
  for greasing

1 tbsp strong black coffee

4 eggs

2 egg yolks

115 g/4 oz caster sugar

40 g/1½ oz plain flour

2 tsp ground cinnamon

85 g/3 oz ground almonds

chocolate-covered coffee
  beans, to decorate

SYRUP

300 ml/10 fl oz strong black
  coffee

115 g/4 oz caster sugar

1 cinnamon stick

STEP 1. Preheat the oven to 190°C/375°F/Gas Mark 5. Grease a 20-cm/8-inch round cake tin and line with baking paper. Put the chocolate, butter and coffee into a heatproof bowl set over a saucepan of gently simmering water and heat until melted. Stir to blend, then remove from the heat and leave to cool slightly.

STEP 2. Put the eggs, egg yolks and sugar into a mixing bowl and whisk together until thick and pale. Sift in the flour and cinnamon. Add the almonds and the chocolate mixture and fold in carefully. Spoon the mixture into the prepared tin. Bake in the preheated oven for 35 minutes, or until a skewer inserted into the centre comes out clean. Leave to cool in the tin for 5 minutes, then turn out onto a wire rack and leave to cool completely.

STEP 3. Meanwhile, make the syrup. Put the coffee, sugar and cinnamon stick into a heavy-based saucepan and heat over a low heat, stirring, until the sugar has dissolved. Increase the heat, bring to the boil and boil for 5 minutes, or until reduced and slightly thickened. Set aside and keep warm. Pierce the surface of the cake with a cocktail stick, then drizzle over half the coffee syrup. Decorate with chocolate-covered coffee beans and serve with the remaining coffee syrup.

chocolate gateau

Serves 10

Difficulty: Medium

Prep: 45 mins, plus 2 hours chilling, and cooling

Cook: 55 mins–1 hour 5 mins

INGREDIENTS

225 g/8 oz butter, softened,
plus extra for greasing

225 g/8 oz golden
caster sugar

4 eggs, beaten

225 g/8 oz self-raising flour

55 g/2 oz cocoa powder

milk (optional)

FILLING

250 ml/9 fl oz whipping
cream

225 g/8 oz white chocolate,
broken into pieces

FROSTING

350 g/12 oz plain chocolate,
broken into pieces

115 g/4 oz butter

100 ml/3½ fl oz
double cream

TO DECORATE

115 g/4 oz plain
chocolate caraque

2 tsp icing sugar and cocoa
powder, mixed

STEP 1. To make the filling, put the whipping cream into a saucepan and heat to almost boiling. Put the white chocolate into a food processor and chop. With the motor running, pour in the hot cream and process for 10–15 seconds until smooth. Transfer to a bowl, leave to cool, then cover with clingfilm and chill in the refrigerator for 2 hours, or until firm. Whip until soft peaks just hold.

STEP 2. Preheat the oven to 180°C/350°F/Gas Mark 4. Grease a 20-cm/8-inch round deep cake tin and line the base with baking paper. Put the butter and sugar into a mixing bowl and cream together until light and fluffy. Add the eggs, one at a time, beating well after each addition. Sift the flour and cocoa powder into a bowl, then fold into the mixture, adding a little milk, if necessary, to make a dropping consistency. Spoon the batter into the prepared tin and bake in the preheated oven for 45–50 minutes until a skewer inserted into the centre comes out clean. Leave to cool in the tin for 5 minutes, then turn out onto a wire rack and leave to cool completely.

STEP 3. To make the frosting, put the plain chocolate into a heatproof bowl set over a saucepan of gently simmering water and heat until melted. Stir in the butter and double cream. Leave to cool, stirring occasionally. Slice the cake horizontally into three layers and sandwich them together with the filling. Cover the top and sides of the cake with the frosting. Arrange the chocolate caraque over the top. Sift over the icing sugar and cocoa powder mixture.

chocolate rum torte

Serves 8

Difficulty: Medium

Prep: 40 mins, plus cooling and setting
Cook: 50 mins

INGREDIENTS

70 g/2½ oz plain chocolate,
  broken into pieces

2 tbsp milk

175 g/6 oz plain white flour

1 tbsp baking powder

175 g/6 oz unsalted butter,
  softened, plus extra
  for greasing

175 g/6 oz dark
  muscovado sugar

3 eggs, beaten

1 tsp vanilla extract

milk chocolate curls
  or grated chocolate,
  to decorate

FROSTING

225 g/8 oz plain chocolate,
  broken into pieces

225 ml/8 fl oz double cream

2 tbsp dark rum

STEP 1. Preheat the oven to 180°C/350°F/Gas Mark 4. Grease three 18-cm/7-inch sandwich tins and line with baking paper.

STEP 2. Put the chocolate and milk into a small saucepan and heat gently, without boiling, until melted. Stir and remove from the heat.

STEP 3. Sift the flour and baking powder into a mixing bowl and add the butter, sugar, eggs and vanilla extract. Beat well until smooth, then stir in the chocolate mixture.

STEP 4. Divide the mixture between the prepared tins and bake in the preheated oven for 40 minutes or until springy to the touch. Leave to cool in the tins for 5 minutes, then turn out onto wire racks and leave to cool completely.

STEP 5. To make the frosting, put the chocolate into a small saucepan with the cream and rum and heat over a low heat until the chocolate has melted. Remove from the heat and leave to cool, stirring occasionally, until the mixture has a spreadable consistency.

STEP 6. Sandwich the cakes together with about a third of the frosting, then spread the remainder over the top and sides of the cake, swirling with a palette knife. Sprinkle with chocolate curls and leave to set.

chocolate brownie cake

Serves 10

Difficulty: Medium

Prep: 30 mins, plus cooling
Cook: 35–40 mins

INGREDIENTS

200 g/7 oz butter,
  plus extra for greasing

115 g/4 oz plain chocolate,
  broken into pieces

280 g/10 oz granulated sugar

115 g/4 oz light muscovado
  sugar

4 eggs, beaten

175 g/6 oz plain flour

1 tsp vanilla extract

pinch of salt

75 g/2¾ oz dried cranberries

75 g/2¾ oz toasted flaked
  almonds, plus extra to
  decorate

FROSTING

115 g/4 oz plain chocolate

25 g/1 oz butter

225 g/8 oz icing sugar

3–4 tbsp milk

STEP 1. Preheat the oven to 180°C/350°F/Gas Mark 4. Grease two 18-cm/7-inch round cake tins and line the bases with baking paper.

STEP 2. Put the butter and chocolate into a heavy-based saucepan and heat over a low heat, stirring frequently, until melted. Remove from the heat and stir until smooth. Transfer the mixture to a mixing bowl, add the granulated sugar and muscovado sugar, stir well, then leave to cool for 10 minutes.

STEP 3. Gradually add the eggs to the cooled chocolate mixture, beating well after each addition. Stir in the flour, vanilla extract and salt. Stir in the cranberries and flaked almonds and mix, then divide between the prepared tins. Bake in the preheated oven for 25–30 minutes or until springy to the touch. Leave to cool in the tins for 5 minutes, then turn out onto wire racks and leave to cool completely.

STEP 4. To make the frosting, put the chocolate and butter into a heavy-based saucepan over a low heat and heat, stirring, until melted. Gradually beat in the icing sugar with enough milk to give a smooth spreading consistency. Use a little of the frosting to sandwich the two cakes together, then spread the remainder over the top and sides, swirling the top to give a decorative effect. Sprinkle the flaked almonds over the top to decorate.

chocolate & walnut cake

Serves 8

Difficulty: Medium

Prep: 35 mins, plus cooling
Cook: 40–45 mins

INGREDIENTS

4 eggs

125 g/4½ oz caster sugar

75 g/2¾ oz plain chocolate,
  broken into pieces

125 g/4½ oz plain flour

1 tbsp cocoa powder

25 g/1 oz butter, melted,
  plus extra for greasing

115 g/4 oz walnuts,
  finely chopped

walnut halves, to decorate

FROSTING

75 g/2¾ oz plain chocolate,
  broken into pieces

115 g/4 oz butter

175 g/6 oz icing sugar

2 tbsp milk

STEP 1. Preheat the oven to 160°C/325°F/Gas Mark 3. Grease an 18-cm/7-inch round cake tin and line with baking paper.

STEP 2. Put the eggs and caster sugar into a mixing bowl and beat with a hand-held electric mixer for 10 minutes, or until foamy and the beaters leave a trail when lifted. Put the chocolate into a heatproof bowl set over a saucepan of gently simmering water and heat until melted. Remove the bowl from the pan.

STEP 3. Sift the flour and cocoa powder together and fold into the egg and sugar mixture. Fold in the melted butter, melted chocolate and chopped walnuts. Pour into the prepared tin and bake in the preheated oven for 30–35 minutes, or until springy to the touch. Leave to cool in the tin for 5 minutes, then turn out onto a wire rack and leave to cool completely.

STEP 4. To make the frosting, put the chocolate into a heatproof bowl set over a saucepan of gently simmering water and heat until melted. Leave to cool slightly. Put the butter, icing sugar and milk into a bowl and beat until pale and fluffy. Add the chocolate and whisk to combine.

STEP 5. Cut the cake horizontally into two layers. Place the bottom half on a serving plate, spread with half the frosting and put the other half on top. Spread the remaining frosting over the top of the cake. Decorate with walnut halves.

chocolate orange cake

Serves 8–10

Difficulty: Medium

Prep: 40 mins, plus cooling and setting
Cook: 45 mins

INGREDIENTS

2 small oranges

85 g/3 oz plain chocolate

250 g/9 oz self-raising flour

1½ tsp baking powder

175 g/6 oz butter, softened,
  plus extra for greasing

200 g/7 oz caster sugar

3 eggs, beaten

TOPPING

175 g/6 oz icing sugar

2 tbsp orange juice

55 g/2 oz plain chocolate,
  broken into pieces

STEP 1. Preheat the oven to 160°C/325°F/Gas Mark 3. Grease an 850-ml/1½-pint ring tin.

STEP 2. Grate the rind from one of the oranges and set aside. Pare the rind from the other orange and set aside. Cut the skin and pith from the oranges, then cut the oranges into segments by cutting down between the membranes with a sharp knife. Chop the segments into small pieces, reserving as much juice as possible. Coarsely grate the chocolate.

STEP 3. Sift the flour and baking powder into a mixing bowl. Add the butter, sugar, eggs, grated orange rind and any reserved juice and beat until smooth. Fold in the chopped oranges and grated chocolate. Spoon the mixture into the prepared tin and bake in the preheated oven for 40 minutes, or until well risen. Leave to cool in the tin for 5 minutes, then turn out onto a wire rack and leave to cool completely.

STEP 4. To make the topping, sift the icing sugar into a bowl and stir in enough orange juice to give a coating consistency. Using a spoon, drizzle the icing over the cake. Put the chocolate into a heatproof bowl set over a saucepan of gently simmering water and heat until melted. Drizzle the melted chocolate over the cake. Cut the reserved pared orange rind into thin strips and scatter over the cake. Leave to set before serving.

chocolate & cherry gateau

Serves 8

Difficulty: Easy

Prep: 30 mins, plus cooling
Cook: 25–30 mins

INGREDIENTS

150 g/5½ oz plain white flour

2 tbsp cocoa powder

1 tbsp baking powder

175 g/6 oz unsalted butter,
  softened, plus extra
  for greasing

175 g/6 oz golden
  caster sugar

3 eggs, beaten

1 tsp vanilla extract

2 tbsp milk

3 tbsp kirsch or brandy
  (optional)

grated chocolate and fresh
  whole cherries, to decorate

FILLING & TOPPING

450 ml/16 fl oz double or
  whipping cream

2 tbsp icing sugar

225 g/8 oz fresh dark red
  cherries, stoned

STEP 1. Preheat the oven to 180°C/350°F/Gas Mark 4. Grease two 20-cm/8-inch sandwich tins and line the bases with baking paper.

STEP 2. Sift the flour, cocoa powder and baking powder into a mixing bowl and add the butter, caster sugar, eggs and vanilla extract. Beat until smooth, then stir in the milk.

STEP 3. Divide the mixture between the prepared tins and smooth the tops with a palette knife. Bake in the preheated oven for 25–30 minutes, or until risen and firm to the touch. Leave to cool in the tins for 2–3 minutes, then turn out onto wire racks and leave to cool completely.

STEP 4. Sprinkle the cooled cakes with the kirsch, if using. To make the filling and topping, whip the cream with the icing sugar until thick, then spread about a third over the top of one of the cakes. Scatter the cherries over the cream and place the second cake on top.

STEP 5. Spread the remaining cream over the top and sides of the cake and decorate with grated chocolate and fresh whole cherries.

chocolate madeira cake

Serves 8–10

Difficulty: Medium

Prep: 30 mins, plus cooling
Cook: 50–55 mins

INGREDIENTS

55 g/2 oz self-raising flour

1 tsp baking powder

115 g/4 oz butter, softened,
  plus extra for greasing

115 g/4 oz caster sugar

3 eggs, beaten

25 g/1 oz ground almonds

115 g/4 oz drinking
  chocolate powder

icing sugar, sifted, for
  dusting

ICING

225 g/8 oz icing sugar

1½ tbsp cocoa powder

2 tbsp butter

3–4 tbsp hot water

STEP 1. Preheat the oven to 180°C/350°F/Gas Mark 4. Grease an 18-cm/7-inch round cake tin and line the base with baking paper. Sift the flour and baking powder into a bowl and set aside.

STEP 2. Put the butter and sugar into a mixing bowl and cream together until light and fluffy, then gradually beat in the eggs, adding a little of the flour after each addition. When all the eggs have been incorporated, stir in the remaining flour and the ground almonds. Sift the drinking chocolate powder into the mixture and lightly stir.

STEP 3. Spoon the mixture into the prepared tin. Bake in the preheated oven for 50–55 minutes, or until a skewer inserted into the centre comes out clean. Leave to cool in the tin for 10 minutes, then turn out onto a wire rack and leave to cool completely.

STEP 4. To make the icing, sift together the icing sugar and cocoa powder into a mixing bowl and make a well in the centre. Add the butter to the well with sufficient hot water to mix to a smooth, spreadable icing. Coat the top and sides of the cake with icing, swirling it to give a decorative effect. Dust with icing sugar.

chocolate heart cake

Serves 12

Difficulty: Medium

Prep: 35 mins, plus cooling
Cook: 30–35 mins

INGREDIENTS

175 g/6 oz self-raising flour

2 tsp baking powder

55 g/2 oz cocoa powder

3 eggs

140 g/5 oz light
    muscovado sugar

150 ml/5 fl oz sunflower oil,
    plus extra for oiling

150 ml/5 fl oz single cream

fresh mint sprigs, to decorate

FILLING & TOPPING

225 g/8 oz plain chocolate

250 ml/9 fl oz double cream

3 tbsp seedless
    raspberry jam

200 g/7 oz fresh or frozen
    raspberries

STEP 1. Preheat the oven to 180°C/350°F/Gas Mark 4. Oil a 20-cm/8-inch heart-shaped cake tin and line the base with baking paper. Sift the flour, baking powder and cocoa powder into a mixing bowl. Put the eggs, sugar, oil and single cream into a separate bowl and beat together. Make a well in the dry ingredients, add the egg mixture, then stir to mix thoroughly, beating to a smooth batter.

STEP 2. Pour the mixture into the prepared tin and bake in the preheated oven for 25–30 minutes, or until risen and firm to the touch. Leave to cool in the tin for 10 minutes, then turn out onto a wire rack and leave to cool completely. To make the filling and topping, put the chocolate and double cream into a saucepan over a low heat and heat, stirring, until melted. Remove from the heat and stir until the mixture is beginning to thicken.

STEP 3. Use a sharp knife to cut the cake in half horizontally. Spread the cut surface of each half with the raspberry jam, then top with about three tablespoons of the chocolate mixture. Scatter half the raspberries over the base and replace the top, pressing lightly. Spread the remaining chocolate mixture over the top and sides of the cake, swirling with a palette knife. Top with the remaining raspberries and decorate with mint sprigs.

chocolate & vanilla cake

Serves 8

Difficulty: Easy

Prep: 30 mins, plus cooling
Cook: 45–50 mins

INGREDIENTS

55 g/2 oz plain chocolate,
  broken into pieces

3 tbsp milk

70 g/2½ oz unsalted butter,
  plus extra for greasing

85 g/3 oz caster sugar

1 egg, beaten

3 tbsp soured cream

115 g/4 oz self-raising flour,
  plus extra for dusting

½ tsp baking powder

½ tsp vanilla extract

STEP 1. Preheat the oven to 160°C/325°F/Gas Mark 3. Grease a 450-g/1-lb loaf tin and line the base with baking paper. Dust a little flour around the inside of the tin, shaking out the excess.

STEP 2. Put the chocolate and the milk into a heatproof bowl set over a saucepan of simmering water and heat until just melted. Remove from the heat.

STEP 3. Put the butter and sugar into a mixing bowl and cream together until light and fluffy. Beat in the egg and soured cream. Sift in the flour and baking powder, then fold in lightly and evenly using a metal spoon.

STEP 4. Spoon half the mixture into a separate bowl and stir in the chocolate mixture. Add the vanilla extract to the plain mixture.

STEP 5. Spoon the chocolate and vanilla mixtures alternately into the prepared tin, lightly swirling with a knife or skewer for a marbled effect. Bake in the preheated oven for 40–45 minutes, or until well risen and firm to the touch.

STEP 6. Leave to cool in the tin for 10 minutes, then turn out onto a wire rack and leave to cool completely.

chocolate poppy seed cake

Serves 4

Difficulty: Medium

Prep: 35 mins, plus 1 hour chilling
Cook: 50 mins

INGREDIENTS

PASTRY

140 g/5 oz butter, softened

3 heaped tbsp caster sugar

pinch of salt

1 egg

200 g/7 oz flour, plus extra
  for dusting

FILLING

140 g/5 oz ground
  poppy seeds

6 tbsp milk

115 g/4 oz granulated sugar

55 g/2 oz plain chocolate,
  grated

55 g/2 oz raisins

55 g/2 oz mixed peel,
  chopped

55 g/2 oz blanched almonds,
  grated

1 egg, beaten

1 tbsp caster sugar

1 tbsp whole poppy seeds

STEP 1. To make the pastry, put the butter, sugar and salt into a mixing bowl and cream together, add the egg, then stir in the flour and just enough cold water to make a soft dough. Cover with clingfilm and chill in the refrigerator for 1 hour.

STEP 2. Preheat the oven to 160°C/325°F/Gas Mark 3. To make the filling, put the poppy seeds and milk into a saucepan and bring to a simmer, then simmer, stirring, for 2 minutes. Remove from the heat and stir in the granulated sugar, chocolate, raisins, mixed peel and almonds. Set aside 1 teaspoon of the beaten egg and beat the remainder into the mixture.

STEP 3. Thinly roll out the pastry on a lightly floured work surface and cut out four 20-cm/8-inch rounds. Place one round in a 20-cm/8-inch loose-based tart tin and spread over one third of the filling. Repeat the layers, finishing with the last pastry round. Press the edges together very lightly, then make a hole in the centre with the handle of a wooden spoon.

STEP 4. Brush the cake with the reserved beaten egg, then sprinkle with the caster sugar and whole poppy seeds. Bake in the preheated oven for about 45 minutes. Serve warm or cold.

chocolate truffle torte

Serves 10

Difficulty: Medium

Prep: 40 mins, plus cooling and chilling
Cook: 17–20 mins

INGREDIENTS

butter, for greasing

50 g/1¾ oz caster sugar

2 eggs

40 g/1¼ oz plain flour

25 g/1 oz cocoa powder

4 tbsp strong black coffee

2 tbsp brandy

cocoa powder and icing
    sugar, to decorate

TRUFFLE FILLING

600 ml/1 pint whipping
    cream

425 g/15 oz plain chocolate,
    broken into pieces

STEP 1. Preheat the oven to 220°C/425°F/Gas Mark 7. Grease a 23-cm/9-inch round, loose-based cake tin and line with baking paper. Put the sugar and eggs into a heatproof bowl set over a saucepan of gently simmering water. Whisk together until pale and resembling the texture of mousse. Remove from the heat. Sift in the flour and cocoa powder and gently fold into the mixture. Pour into the prepared tin and bake in the preheated oven for 7–10 minutes, or until risen and firm to the touch. Leave to cool in the tin for 10 minutes, then turn out onto a wire rack and leave to cool completely.

STEP 2. Wash and dry the cake tin and replace the cooled cake in the tin. Mix the coffee and brandy together and brush over the cake. To make the truffle filling, put the cream into a bowl and whip until soft peaks just hold. Put the chocolate into a heatproof bowl set over a saucepan of gently simmering water and heat until melted. Remove from the heat. Carefully fold the cooled chocolate into the cream, then pour the mixture over the sponge. Chill in the refrigerator until set.

STEP 3. To decorate the torte, sift cocoa powder over the top and carefully remove from the tin. Using strips of card or baking paper, sift bands of icing sugar over the torte to create a striped pattern.

mocha layer cake

Serves 8

Difficulty: Medium

Prep: 40 mins, plus cooling
Cook: 35–45 mins

INGREDIENTS

butter, for greasing

250 g/9 oz self-raising flour

¼ tsp baking powder

4 tbsp cocoa powder

115 g/4 oz caster sugar

2 eggs

2 tbsp golden syrup

150 ml/5 fl oz sunflower oil

150 ml/5 fl oz milk

FILLING

1 tsp instant coffee powder

1 tbsp boiling water

300 ml/10 fl oz
  double cream

2 tbsp icing sugar

TO DECORATE

50 g/1¾ oz chocolate
  shavings

75 g/2¾ oz marbled
  chocolate caraque

sifted icing sugar

STEP 1. Preheat the oven to 180°C/350°F/Gas Mark 4. Lightly grease three 18-cm/7-inch sandwich tins.

STEP 2. Sift the flour, baking powder and cocoa powder into a large mixing bowl. Stir in the sugar. Make a well in the centre and stir in the eggs, golden syrup, oil and milk. Beat with a wooden spoon, gradually mixing in the dry ingredients, until smooth. Divide the mixture between the prepared tins.

STEP 3. Bake in the preheated oven for 35–45 minutes, or until springy to the touch. Leave the cakes to cool in the tins for 5 minutes, then turn out onto wire racks and leave to cool completely.

STEP 4. To make the filling, dissolve the coffee powder in the water and put into a mixing bowl with the cream and icing sugar. Whip until it just holds its shape. Use half of the mixture to sandwich the three cakes together. Spread the remaining mixture over the top and side of the cake. Lightly press the chocolate shavings around the side of the cake.

STEP 5. Transfer to a serving plate. Lay the caraque over the top of the cake. Cut a few thin strips of baking paper and place on top of the caraque. Lightly dust with icing sugar, then carefully remove the paper.

dotty chocolate chip cake

Serves 10

Difficulty: Easy

Prep: 25 mins, plus cooling
Cook: 45–50 mins

INGREDIENTS

175 g/6 oz butter, softened,
  plus extra for greasing

175 g/6 oz caster sugar

3 eggs, beaten

175 g/6 oz plain flour

1 tsp baking powder

2 tbsp cocoa powder

55 g/2 oz white
  chocolate chips

40 g/1½ oz sugar-coated
  chocolate drops, to
  decorate

FROSTING

175 g/6 oz milk chocolate or
  plain chocolate

100 g/3½ oz unsalted butter
  or margarine

1 tbsp golden syrup

STEP 1. Preheat the oven to 160°C/325°F/Gas Mark 3. Grease a 20-cm/8-inch round cake tin and line the base with baking paper.

STEP 2. Put the butter, sugar, eggs, flour, baking powder and cocoa powder into a mixing bowl and beat until just smooth. Stir in the chocolate chips, mixing evenly.

STEP 3. Spoon the mixture into the prepared tin. Bake in the preheated oven for 40–45 minutes until risen and firm to the touch. Leave to cool in the tin for 5 minutes, then turn out onto a wire rack and leave to cool completely.

STEP 4. To make the frosting, put the chocolate, butter and golden syrup into a saucepan over a low heat and stir until just melted and smooth.

STEP 5. Remove from the heat and leave to cool until it begins to thicken enough to leave a trail when the spoon is lifted. Pour the frosting over the top of the cake, allowing it to drizzle down the side. Arrange the chocolate drops over the top of the cake.

marble cake

Serves 10

Difficulty: Easy

Prep: 25 mins, plus cooling and setting
Cook: 1 hour–1 hour 10 mins

INGREDIENTS

55 g/2 oz plain chocolate,
  broken into pieces

1 tbsp strong black coffee

280 g/10 oz self-raising flour

1 tsp baking powder

225 g/8 oz butter, softened,
  plus extra for greasing

225 g/8 oz caster sugar

4 eggs, beaten

50 g/1¾ oz ground almonds

2 tbsp milk

1 tsp vanilla extract

ICING

125 g/4½ oz plain chocolate,
  broken into pieces

2 tbsp butter

2 tbsp water

STEP 1. Preheat the oven to 180°C/350°F/Gas Mark 4. Grease a 1.7-litre/3-pint ring tin. Put the chocolate and coffee into a heatproof bowl set over a saucepan of gently simmering water and heat until the chocolate has melted. Leave to cool. Sift the flour and baking powder into a mixing bowl. Add the butter, sugar, eggs, ground almonds and milk. Beat well until smooth.

STEP 2. Transfer one half of the mixture to a separate bowl and stir in the vanilla extract. Stir the cooled chocolate into the other half of the mixture. Drop spoonfuls of the two mixtures alternately into the ring mould, then drag a skewer through to create a marbled effect. Smooth the top. Bake in the preheated oven for 50 mins–1 hour until risen and a skewer inserted into the centre comes out clean. Leave to cool in the mould for 5 minutes, then turn out onto a wire rack and leave to cool completely.

STEP 3. To make the icing, put the chocolate, butter and water into a heatproof bowl set over a saucepan of gently simmering water and heat until melted. Remove from the heat, stir and pour over the cake, working quickly to coat the top and sides. Leave to set before serving.

*Note: You can use a fluted or plain ring tin for this recipe – the fluted finish is good for special occasion cakes.

gooey orange chocolate chip cake

Serves 6

Difficulty: Medium

Prep: 35 mins
Cook: 40–45 mins

INGREDIENTS

2 oranges

175 g/6 oz plain white flour

2 tsp baking powder

175 g/6 oz butter, softened,
  plus extra for greasing

175 g/6 oz golden caster
  sugar

3 eggs, beaten

1 tsp vanilla extract

100 g/3½ oz plain
  chocolate chips

SAUCE

85 g/3 oz plain chocolate,
  broken into pieces

40 g/1½ oz butter

3 tbsp orange juice

STEP 1. Preheat the oven to 180°C/350°F/Gas Mark 4. Grease a 23-cm/9-inch square cake tin and line with baking paper.

STEP 2. Finely grate the rind from one of the oranges and reserve. Use a sharp knife to cut off all the peel and white pith from both oranges and carefully remove the segments, reserving any spare juices to add to the sauce. Chop half the segments into small pieces.

STEP 3. Sift the flour and baking powder into a large bowl and add the butter, sugar, eggs and vanilla extract. Beat well until smooth, then stir in the orange rind and chopped orange.

STEP 4. Spoon the mixture into the prepared tin and smooth the surface with a palette knife. Sprinkle the chocolate chips over the top, spreading to the edges with a palette knife. Bake in the preheated oven for 35–40 minutes, or until well risen, golden brown and firm to the touch.

STEP 5. To make the sauce, put the chocolate, butter and orange juice into a saucepan and gently heat, stirring, until melted and smooth. Serve the cake warm, topped with the reserved orange segments and with the sauce spooned over the top.

no-bake raisin biscuit cake

Makes about 20 pieces

Difficulty: Easy

Prep: 15 mins, plus 5 mins cooling and 1–2 hours chilling
Cook: 10 mins

INGREDIENTS

100 g/3½ oz butter, plus
    extra for greasing

25 g/1 oz cocoa powder

200 g/7 oz digestive biscuits,
    crushed

85 g/3 oz dried cranberries
    or raisins

1 egg, beaten

125 g/4 oz milk chocolate,
    broken into squares

STEP 1. Lightly grease a 450-g/1-lb loaf tin and line it with baking paper.

STEP 2. Put the butter and cocoa powder into a saucepan over a low heat and heat until melted and well combined. Remove from the heat and stir in the crushed biscuits and cranberries. Leave to cool for 5 minutes. Add the egg and mix well together.

STEP 3. Spoon the mixture into the prepared tin, pressing down well with the back of the spoon.

STEP 4. Put the chocolate into a heatproof bowl set over a saucepan of gently simmering water. Heat until melted, then spread over the top of the cake. Leave to set in the refrigerator for 1–2 hours. Cut into squares and serve.

*Note: For extra crunch, you could add 50 g/2¾ oz chopped hazelnuts or pistachio nuts with the dried fruit in Step 2.

no-bake chocolate cake

Serves 6–8

Difficulty: Easy

Prep: 10 mins, plus 1–2 hours chilling
Cook: 5 mins

INGREDIENTS

225 g/8 oz plain chocolate

225 g/8 oz butter, plus extra
for greasing

3 tbsp black coffee

55 g/2 oz soft light
brown sugar

a few drops of
vanilla extract

225 g/8 oz digestive biscuits,
crushed

85 g/3 oz raisins

85 g/3 oz walnuts, chopped

STEP 1. Lightly grease a 450-g/1-lb loaf tin and line with baking paper.

STEP 2. Put the chocolate, butter, coffee, sugar and vanilla extract into a saucepan over a low heat and stir until the chocolate and butter have melted, the sugar has dissolved and the mixture is well combined.

STEP 3. Stir in the crushed biscuits, raisins and walnuts. Spoon the mixture into the prepared tin. Leave to set for 1–2 hours in the refrigerator, then turn out and cut into thin slices to serve.

*Note: You can store this cake in the fridge in an airtight container for up to 1 week, or in the freezer for 1 month, tightly wrapped in a freezer-proof polythene bag. Unwrap and thaw in the fridge for 3–5 hours before slicing.

cookies, muffins & cupcakes

mega chip cookies

Makes 12

Difficulty: Easy

Prep: 20 mins, plus cooling
Cook: 12–15 mins

INGREDIENTS

225 g/8 oz butter, softened

140 g/5 oz caster sugar

1 egg yolk, beaten

2 tsp vanilla extract

225 g/8 oz plain flour

55 g/2 oz cocoa powder

pinch of salt

85 g/3 oz milk
   chocolate chips

85 g/3 oz white
   chocolate chips

115 g/4 oz plain chocolate,
   roughly chopped

STEP 1. Preheat the oven to 190°C/375°F/Gas Mark 5. Line two baking sheets with baking paper.

STEP 2. Put the butter and sugar into a mixing bowl and cream together, then beat in the egg yolk and vanilla extract. Sift together the flour, cocoa powder and salt into the mixture, add the milk chocolate chips and white chocolate chips and stir well to combine.

STEP 3. Make 12 balls of the mixture, place them on the prepared baking sheets, spaced well apart, and flatten slightly. Press the plain chocolate pieces into the cookies.

STEP 4. Bake in the preheated oven for 12–15 minutes. Leave to cool on the baking sheets for 5–10 minutes, then transfer to wire racks and leave to cool completely.

white chocolate cookies

Makes 24

Difficulty: Easy
Prep: 20 mins, plus cooling
Cook: 10–12 mins

INGREDIENTS

115 g/4 oz butter, softened

115 g/4 oz soft brown sugar

1 egg, beaten

250 g/9 oz self-raising flour

pinch of salt

125 g/4½ oz white chocolate, roughly chopped

50 g/1¾ oz Brazil nuts, chopped

STEP 1. Preheat the oven to 190°C/375°F/Gas Mark 5. Line four baking sheets with baking paper.

STEP 2. Put the butter and sugar into a mixing bowl and cream together, then beat in the egg. Sift the flour and salt into the mixture, add the chocolate and nuts and stir until thoroughly combined.

STEP 3. Make 24 balls out of the mixture, place on the prepared baking sheets, spaced well apart, and flatten slightly. Bake in the preheated oven for 10–12 minutes.

STEP 4. Leave to cool on the baking sheets for 5–10 minutes, then transfer the cookies to wire racks and leave to cool completely.

*Note: Check the expiry date on your white chocolate before using. It has a much shorter shelf life – about 6 months – than either milk chocolate or plain chocolate.

chocolate orange cookies

Makes about 30

Difficulty: Medium

Prep: 25 mins, plus cooling and setting
Cook: 15–17 mins

INGREDIENTS

90 g/3¼ oz butter, softened

60 g/2¼ oz caster sugar

1 egg

1 tbsp milk

280 g/10 oz plain flour, plus
  extra for dusting

2 tbsp cocoa powder

ICING

175 g/6 oz icing sugar

3 tbsp orange juice

a little plain chocolate,
  broken into pieces

STEP 1. Preheat the oven to 180°C/350°F/Gas Mark 4.
Line four baking sheets with baking paper.

STEP 2. Put the butter and sugar into a mixing bowl
and cream together, then beat in the egg and milk and
stir until thoroughly combined. Sift the flour and cocoa
powder into the bowl and gradually mix to a soft dough.

STEP 3. Roll out the dough on a lightly floured work
surface to a thickness of about 5 mm/¼ inch. Cut out
rounds with a 5-cm/2-inch fluted round cutter and place
them on the prepared baking sheets, spaced well apart,
and flatten slightly. Bake in the preheated oven for
10–12 minutes, or until golden brown. Leave to cool on
the baking sheets for a few minutes, then transfer to wire
racks and leave to cool completely.

STEP 4. To make the icing, sift the icing sugar into a bowl
and stir in enough orange juice to mix to a thin icing that
will coat the back of the spoon. Place a spoonful of icing
in the centre of each cookie and leave to set.

STEP 5. Put the chocolate into a heatproof bowl set over
a saucepan of gently simmering water and heat until
melted, then remove the bowl from the pan. Drizzle thin
lines of melted chocolate over the cookies and leave to
set before serving.

cappuccino cookies

Makes about 30

Difficulty: Medium

Prep: 30 mins, plus 30 mins–1 hour chilling, and cooling and setting
Cook: 15–20 mins

INGREDIENTS

225 g/8 oz butter, softened

140 g/5 oz caster sugar

1 egg yolk, beaten

2 sachets instant cappuccino powder mixed with 1 tbsp hot water

280 g/10 oz plain flour

pinch of salt

175 g/6 oz white chocolate, broken into pieces

cocoa powder, for dusting

STEP 1. Put the butter and sugar into a mixing bowl and cream together, then beat in the egg yolk and the cappuccino mixture. Sift together the flour and salt into the bowl and stir until thoroughly combined. Halve the dough, wrap in clingfilm and chill in the refrigerator for 30 minutes–1 hour.

STEP 2. Preheat the oven to 190°C/375°F/Gas Mark 5. Line four baking sheets with baking paper.

STEP 3. Unwrap the dough and roll out between two sheets of baking paper. Stamp out cookies with a 6-cm/2½-inch round cutter, place them on the prepared baking sheets, spaced well apart, and flatten slightly.

STEP 4. Bake in the preheated oven for 10–12 minutes until golden brown. Leave to cool on the baking sheets for 5–10 minutes, then carefully transfer to wire racks and leave to cool completely.

STEP 5. When the cookies are cool, place the wire racks over a sheet of baking paper. Put the chocolate into a heatproof bowl set over a saucepan of gently simmering water and heat until melted. Remove the bowl from the pan and leave to cool, then spoon the chocolate over the cookies. Gently tap the wire racks to level the surface and leave to set. Lightly dust with cocoa powder.

chocolate & coffee wholemeal cookies

Makes 24

Difficulty: Easy

Prep: 20 mins, plus cooling
Cook: 16–18 mins

INGREDIENTS

175 g/6 oz butter

200 g/7 oz soft light
  brown sugar

1 egg

70 g/2½ oz plain flour

1 tsp bicarbonate of soda

pinch of salt

70 g/2½ oz wholemeal flour

1 tbsp bran

225 g/8 oz plain
  chocolate chips

185 g/6½ oz rolled oats

1 tbsp strong coffee

100 g/3½ oz hazelnuts,
  toasted and roughly
  chopped

STEP 1. Preheat the oven to 190°C/375°F/Gas Mark 5.
Line four baking sheets with baking paper.

STEP 2. Put the butter and sugar into a mixing bowl and
cream together, then beat in the egg. Sift together the
plain flour, bicarbonate of soda and salt into a separate
mixing bowl, then add the wholemeal flour and bran. Mix
in the egg mixture, then stir in the chocolate chips, oats,
coffee and hazelnuts and mix well together.

STEP 3. Make 24 balls of the mixture, place them on the
prepared baking sheets, spaced well apart, and flatten
slightly. Bake in the preheated oven for 16–18 minutes, or
until golden brown. Leave to cool on the baking sheets
for 5–10 minutes, then transfer to wire racks and leave to
cool completely.

chocolate sprinkle cookies

Makes about 30

Difficulty: Medium

Prep: 30 mins, plus 30 mins–1 hour chilling, and cooling and setting
Cook: 15–17 mins

INGREDIENTS

225 g/8 oz butter, softened

140 g/5 oz caster sugar

1 egg yolk, lightly beaten

2 tsp vanilla extract

225 g/8 oz plain flour, plus
  extra for dusting

55 g/2 oz cocoa powder

pinch of salt

200 g/7 oz white chocolate,
  broken into pieces

85 g/3 oz chocolate
  vermicelli, to decorate

STEP 1. Put the butter and sugar into a mixing bowl and cream together, then beat in the egg yolk and vanilla extract. Sift together the flour, cocoa powder and salt into the mixture and stir until thoroughly combined. Halve the dough, wrap in clingfilm and chill in the refrigerator for 30 minutes–1 hour.

STEP 2. Preheat the oven to 190°C/375°F/Gas Mark 5. Line four baking sheets with baking paper.

STEP 3. Unwrap the dough, roll out between two pieces of baking paper to a thickness of about 5 mm/¼ inch and stamp out 30 cookies with a 6–7-cm/2½–2¾-inch fluted round cutter. Place them on the prepared baking sheets, spaced well apart, and flatten slightly.

STEP 4. Bake in the preheated oven for 10–12 minutes. Leave to cool on the baking sheets for 5–10 minutes, then transfer to wire racks and leave to cool completely.

STEP 5. Put the white chocolate into a heatproof bowl set over a saucepan of gently simmering water and heat until melted, then immediately remove the bowl from the pan. Spread the melted chocolate over the cookies. Leave to cool slightly, then sprinkle with the chocolate vermicelli. Leave to cool and set.

nutty drizzle cookies

Makes 24

Difficulty: Easy

Prep: 20 mins, plus cooling

Cook: 17–20 mins

INGREDIENTS

200 g/7 oz butter
  or margarine

275 g/9¾ oz brown sugar

1 egg

140 g/5 oz plain flour, sifted

1 tsp baking powder

1 tsp bicarbonate of soda

125 g/4½ oz rolled oats

1 tbsp bran

1 tbsp wheatgerm

115 g/4 oz mixed nuts,
  toasted and roughly
  chopped

200 g/7 oz plain chocolate
  chips

115 g/4 oz mixed raisins and
  sultanas

175 g/6 oz plain chocolate,
  roughly chopped

STEP 1. Preheat the oven to 180°C/350°F/Gas Mark 4. Line four baking sheets with baking paper.

STEP 2. Put the butter and sugar into a mixing bowl and cream together, then beat in the egg. Add the flour, baking powder, bicarbonate of soda, oats, bran and wheatgerm and mix together until well combined. Finally, stir in the nuts, chocolate chips and dried fruit.

STEP 3. Make 24 balls of the mixture, place them on the prepared baking sheets, spaced well apart, and flatten slightly. Bake in the preheated oven for 12–15 minutes. Leave to cool on the baking sheets for 5–10 minutes, then transfer to wire racks and leave to cool completely.

STEP 4. Put the chocolate pieces into a heatproof bowl set over a saucepan of gently simmering water and heat until melted. Stir the chocolate, then remove the bowl from the pan and leave to cool slightly. Use a spoon to drizzle the chocolate over the cookies, or spoon it into a piping bag and pipe zig-zag lines over them.

viennese fingers

Makes about 16

Difficulty: Medium

Prep: 25 mins, plus cooling and setting
Cook: 15–20 mins

INGREDIENTS

100 g/3½ oz unsalted butter,
  plus extra for greasing

25 g/1 oz golden caster
  sugar

½ tsp vanilla extract

100 g/3½ oz self-raising flour

100 g/3½ oz plain chocolate,
  roughly chopped

STEP 1. Preheat the oven to 160°C/325°F/Gas Mark 3. Lightly grease two baking trays.

STEP 2. Put the butter, sugar and vanilla extract into a mixing bowl and cream together until light and fluffy. Stir in the flour, mixing evenly to a fairly stiff dough.

STEP 3. Spoon the mixture into a piping bag fitted with a large star nozzle and pipe about 16 fingers, each 6 cm/2½ inches long, onto the prepared trays.

STEP 4. Bake in the preheated oven for 10–15 minutes until pale golden. Leave to cool on the trays for 2–3 minutes, then use a palette knife to transfer to wire racks and leave to cool completely.

STEP 5. Put the chocolate into a small heatproof bowl set over a saucepan of gently simmering water and heat until melted. Remove the bowl from the pan. Dip both ends of each biscuit into the chocolate to coat, then place on a sheet of baking paper and leave to set.

chocolate chunk muffins

Makes 12

Difficulty: Easy

Prep: 20 mins
Cook: 20 mins

INGREDIENTS

280 g/10 oz plain white flour

1 tbsp baking powder

pinch of salt

115 g/4 oz caster sugar

175 g/6 oz chocolate chunks

2 eggs, beaten

250 ml/9 fl oz milk

6 tbsp sunflower oil or
   85 g/3 oz butter,
   melted and cooled

1 tsp vanilla extract

STEP 1. Preheat the oven to 200°C/400°F/Gas Mark 6. Line a 12-hole muffin tin with paper cases. Sift the flour, baking powder and salt into a mixing bowl. Stir in the sugar and chocolate chunks.

STEP 2. Put the eggs, milk, oil and vanilla extract into a separate mixing bowl and mix well. Add the wet ingredients to the dry ingredients and gently stir until just combined.

STEP 3. Spoon the mixture into the paper cases and bake in the preheated oven for about 20 minutes until well risen, golden brown and firm to the touch. Serve warm or cold.

*Note: For best results, don't over-mix when adding the wet and dry ingredients. There should still be some flour showing when the muffins go into the oven.

triple chocolate muffins

Makes 12

Difficulty: Easy

Prep: 20 mins

Cook: 20 mins

INGREDIENTS

250 g/9 oz plain flour

25 g/1 oz cocoa powder

2 tsp baking powder

½ tsp bicarbonate of soda

100 g/3½ oz plain
   chocolate chips

100 g/3½ oz white
   chocolate chips

2 eggs, beaten

300 ml/10 fl oz
   soured cream

85 g/3 oz light
   muscovado sugar

85 g/3 oz butter,
   melted and cooled

STEP 1. Preheat the oven to 200°C/400°F/Gas Mark 6. Line a 12-hole muffin tin with paper cases. Sift the flour, cocoa powder, baking powder and bicarbonate of soda into a large bowl, then stir in the plain chocolate chips and white chocolate chips.

STEP 2. Put the eggs, soured cream, sugar and butter into a separate mixing bowl and mix well together. Add the wet ingredients to the dry ingredients and gently stir until just combined.

STEP 3. Spoon the mixture into the paper cases and bake in the preheated oven for 20 minutes, or until well risen and firm to the touch. Serve warm or cold.

chocolate orange muffins

Makes 10

Difficulty: Easy

Prep: 20 mins
Cook: 20–25 mins

INGREDIENTS

125 g/4½ oz self-raising
  white flour

125 g/4½ oz self-raising
  wholemeal flour

25 g/1 oz ground almonds

55 g/2 oz soft brown sugar

grated rind and juice of
  1 orange

175 g/6 oz cream cheese

2 eggs

55 g/2 oz plain
  chocolate chips

STEP 1. Preheat the oven to 190°C/375°F/Gas Mark 5.
Line a 10-hole muffin tin with paper cases.

STEP 2. Sift the white flour and wholemeal flour into a
mixing bowl, then stir in the ground almonds and sugar.

STEP 3. Put the orange rind and juice, cream cheese,
eggs and chocolate chips into a separate mixing bowl
and mix well together. Add the wet ingredients to the dry
ingredients and gently stir until just combined.

STEP 4. Spoon the mixture into the paper cases and bake
in the preheated oven for 20–25 minutes, or until well
risen and golden brown. Serve warm or cold.

spiced chocolate muffins

Makes 12

Difficulty: Easy

Prep: 15 mins
Cook: 25–30 mins

INGREDIENTS

250 g/9 oz plain flour

1 tsp bicarbonate of soda

2 tbsp cocoa powder

1 tsp allspice

200 g/7 oz plain chocolate chips

100 g/3½ oz butter, softened

150 g /5½ oz caster sugar

115 g/4 oz soft light brown sugar

2 eggs

150 ml/5 fl oz soured cream

5 tbsp milk

STEP 1. Preheat the oven to 190°C/375°F/Gas Mark 5. Line a 12-hole muffin tin with paper cases. Sift the flour, bicarbonate of soda, cocoa powder and allspice into a mixing bowl, then stir in the chocolate chips.

STEP 2. Put the butter, caster sugar and brown sugar into a separate mixing bowl and mix well together. Beat in the eggs, soured cream and milk until thoroughly combined. Add the wet mixture to the dry mixture and gently stir until just combined.

STEP 3. Spoon the mixture into the paper cases and bake in the preheated oven for 25–30 minutes, or until well risen and firm to the touch. Serve warm or cold.

*Note: If you prefer, use milk instead of soured cream, replacing the bicarbonate of soda with 1 tablespoon of baking powder.

coffee & cream muffins

Makes 12

Difficulty: Easy

Prep: 30 mins, plus cooling
Cook: 20–25 mins

INGREDIENTS

280 g/10 oz plain white flour

1 tbsp baking powder

pinch of salt

115 g/4 oz soft dark
  brown sugar

2 eggs, beaten

200 ml/7 fl oz double cream

6 tbsp sunflower oil or
  85 g/3 oz butter, melted
  and cooled

2 tbsp instant coffee
  granules mixed with 2 tbsp
  boiling water

300 ml/10 fl oz whipping
  cream

cocoa powder, for dusting

12 chocolate-covered coffee
  beans, to decorate

STEP 1. Preheat the oven to 200°C/400°F/Gas Mark 6. Line a 12-hole muffin tin with paper cases. Sift the flour, baking powder and salt into a mixing bowl, then stir in the sugar.

STEP 2. Put the eggs, double cream, oil and coffee into a separate mixing bowl and mix well together. Add the wet ingredients to the dry ingredients and gently stir until just combined.

STEP 3. Spoon the mixture into the paper cases and bake in the preheated oven for 20–25 minutes, or until golden brown and firm to the touch.

STEP 4. Leave to cool in the tin for 5 minutes, then transfer to a wire rack and leave to cool completely. Just before serving, whip the whipping cream until it holds its shape. Spoon a dollop of the cream on top of each muffin, lightly dust with cocoa powder and top with a chocolate-covered coffee bean.

chocolate butterfly cupcakes

Makes 12

Difficulty: Medium

Prep: 30 mins, plus cooling
Cook: 15 mins

INGREDIENTS

125 g/4½ oz soft margarine

125 g/4½ oz caster sugar

150 g/5½ oz self-raising flour, sifted

2 eggs

2 tbsp cocoa powder

25 g/1 oz plain chocolate, melted

LEMON BUTTERCREAM

100 g/3½ oz butter, softened

225 g/8 oz icing sugar, sifted, plus extra for dusting

grated rind of ½ lemon

1 tbsp lemon juice

STEP 1. Preheat the oven to 180°C/350°F/Gas Mark 4. Line a 12-hole bun tin with paper cases. Put the margarine, caster sugar, flour, eggs and cocoa powder into a mixing bowl and beat until just smooth. Beat in the melted chocolate.

STEP 2. Spoon the mixture into the paper cases, filling them three-quarters full. Bake in the preheated oven for 15 minutes, or until well risen. Transfer to a wire rack and leave to cool completely.

STEP 3. To make the buttercream, put the butter into a mixing bowl and beat until fluffy. Gradually add the icing sugar, lemon rind and lemon juice, beating well after each addition.

STEP 4. Cut the top off each cake with a serrated knife. Cut the cake tops in half. Spread the lemon buttercream over the cut surface of each cake and push the two pieces of cake top into the buttercream to make wings. Dust with icing sugar.

dark & white fudge cupcakes

Makes 20

Difficulty: Medium

Prep: 20 mins, plus cooling
Cook: 30 mins

INGREDIENTS

200 ml/7 fl oz water

85 g/3 oz butter

85 g/3 oz caster sugar

1 tbsp golden syrup

3 tbsp milk

1 tsp vanilla extract

1 tsp bicarbonate of soda

225 g/8 oz plain flour

2 tbsp cocoa powder

FROSTING

50 g/1¾ oz plain chocolate

4 tbsp water

50 g/1¾ oz butter

50 g/1¾ oz white chocolate

350 g/12 oz icing sugar

TO DECORATE

100 g/3½ oz plain
  chocolate shavings

100 g/3½ oz white chocolate
  shavings

STEP 1. Preheat the oven to 180°C/350°F/Gas Mark 4. Line two bun tins with 20 paper cases. Put the water, butter, sugar and golden syrup into a saucepan set over a low heat and stir until the sugar has dissolved, then bring to the boil. Reduce the heat and cook for 5 minutes. Remove from the heat and leave to cool.

STEP 2. Meanwhile, put the milk and vanilla extract into a small bowl. Add the bicarbonate of soda and stir to dissolve. Put the flour and cocoa powder into a mixing bowl and add the syrup mixture. Stir in the milk and vanilla extract and beat until smooth. Spoon the mixture into the paper cases until they are two-thirds full.

STEP 3. Bake the cupcakes in the preheated oven for 20 minutes, or until well risen and firm to the touch. Transfer to wire racks and leave to cool.

STEP 4. To make the frosting, put the plain chocolate, 2 tablespoons of the water and 25 g/1 oz of the butter into a small heatproof bowl set over a saucepan of gently simmering water and heat until the chocolate and butter are melted. Stir until smooth and leave to stand over the pan. Repeat with the white chocolate and the remaining water and butter. Sift half the icing sugar into each bowl and beat until smooth and thick. Top the cupcakes with the frosting. Serve decorated with chocolate shavings.

mocha cupcakes with whipped cream

Makes 20

Difficulty: Easy

Prep: 20 mins, plus cooling
Cook: 25–30 mins

INGREDIENTS

2 tbsp instant espresso
  coffee powder

85 g/3 oz butter

85 g/3 oz caster sugar

1 tbsp clear honey

200 ml/7 fl oz water

225 g/8 oz plain flour

2 tbsp cocoa powder

1 tsp bicarbonate of soda

3 tbsp milk

1 large egg, beaten

TOPPING

225 ml/8 fl oz whipping
  cream

cocoa powder, for dusting

STEP 1. Preheat the oven to 180°C/350°F/Gas Mark 4. Line two shallow bun tins with 20 paper cases. Put the coffee powder, butter, sugar, honey and water into a saucepan over a low heat and stir until the sugar has dissolved. Bring to the boil, then reduce the heat and simmer for 5 minutes. Pour into a large heatproof bowl and leave to cool.

STEP 2. Sift the flour and cocoa powder into the cooled mixture. Put the bicarbonate of soda and milk into a bowl and stir to dissolve, then add to the mixture with the egg and beat until smooth. Spoon into the paper cases.

STEP 3. Bake in the preheated oven for 15–20 minutes, or until well risen and firm to the touch. Transfer the cupcakes to wire racks to and leave to cool completely.

STEP 4. To make the topping, put the cream in a bowl and whip until it holds its shape. Spoon heaped teaspoons of cream on top of each cake, then lightly dust with sifted cocoa powder.

rocky mountain cupcakes

Makes 10

Difficulty: Medium
Prep: 30 mins, plus cooling
Cook: 30–35 mins

INGREDIENTS

140 g/5 oz butter, softened

140 g/5 oz caster sugar

1 tsp vanilla extract

3 eggs, beaten

150 g/5½ oz self-raising flour

55 g/2 oz cocoa powder

TOPPING

105 g/3¾ oz plain chocolate,
  broken into pieces

2 tbsp water

25 g/1 oz butter

175 g/6 oz icing sugar

85 g/3 oz mini marshmallows

40 g/1½ oz walnuts,
  roughly chopped

STEP 1. Preheat the oven to 180°C/350°F/Gas Mark 4. Line a shallow bun tin with 10 paper cases. Put the butter and caster sugar into a mixing bowl and cream together until light and fluffy, then beat in the vanilla extract. Gradually beat in the eggs. Sift in the flour and cocoa powder and fold into the mixture. Spoon the mixture into the paper cases.

STEP 2. Bake in the preheated oven for 20–25 minutes, or until springy to the touch. Transfer to a wire rack to cool completely.

STEP 3. To make the topping, put 50 g/1¾ oz of the chocolate, the water and butter into a small heatproof bowl set over a saucepan of gently simmering water and heat until the chocolate and butter are melted. Stir until smooth and leave to stand over the pan. Sift the icing sugar into the bowl and beat until smooth and thick.

STEP 4. Pipe the mixture on top of each cake to make a peak in the centre. Mix the marshmallows and walnuts together and divide between the cakes, then press down lightly. Put the remaining chocolate into a heatproof bowl set over a saucepan of gently simmering water and heat until melted. Drizzle over the tops of the cakes and leave to set.

hot pecan brownie cupcakes

Makes 6

Difficulty: Medium

Prep: 20 mins, plus 5 mins cooling
Cook: 30–35 mins

INGREDIENTS

115 g/4 oz plain chocolate, broken into pieces

115 g/4 oz butter, plus extra for greasing

2 eggs

115 g/4 oz soft light brown sugar

3 tbsp maple syrup

115 g/4 oz plain flour, sifted

55 g/2 oz pecan nuts, chopped

STEP 1. Preheat the oven to 180°C/350°F/Gas Mark 4. Grease six 150-ml/5-fl oz ovenproof teacups.

STEP 2. Put the chocolate and butter into a heatproof bowl set over a saucepan of gently simmering water and heat, stirring occasionally, until melted. Leave to cool for 5 minutes.

STEP 3. Put the eggs, sugar and maple syrup into a mixing bowl and beat together until well blended. Beat in the chocolate mixture, then fold in the flour and two thirds of the pecan nuts. Pour the mixture into the prepared cups and scatter over the remaining nuts.

STEP 4. Put the cups on a baking sheet and bake in the preheated oven for 25–30 minutes, or until the cupcakes are risen and crisp on top, but still feel slightly wobbly if lightly pressed. Serve warm.

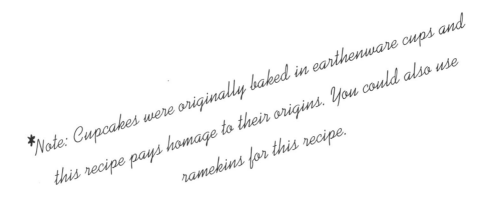

*Note: Cupcakes were originally baked in earthenware cups and this recipe pays homage to their origins. You could also use ramekins for this recipe.

black forest cupcakes

Makes 12

Difficulty: Medium

Prep: 25 mins, plus 10 mins standing, and cooling
Cook: 25–30 mins

INGREDIENTS

85 g/3 oz plain chocolate,
  broken into pieces

1 tsp lemon juice

4 tbsp milk

150 g/5½ oz
  self-raising flour

1 tbsp cocoa powder,
  plus extra for dusting

½ tsp bicarbonate of soda

2 eggs

55 g/2 oz butter, softened

115 g/4 oz soft light
  brown sugar

25 g/1 oz dried sweetened
  sour cherries, chopped

2 tbsp cherry liqueur
  (optional)

150 ml/5 fl oz double cream,
  softly whipped

5 tbsp cherry conserve

STEP 1. Preheat the oven to 180°C/350°F/Gas Mark 4.
Line a shallow bun tin with 12 paper cases.

STEP 2. Put the chocolate into a heatproof bowl set over
a saucepan of gently simmering water and heat until
melted. Add the lemon juice to the milk and leave to
stand for 10 minutes – the milk will curdle a little.

STEP 3. Sift the flour, cocoa powder and bicarbonate of
soda into a mixing bowl. Add the eggs, butter, sugar
and the milk and lemon mixture and beat until smooth.
Fold in the melted chocolate and the cherries. Spoon the
mixture into the paper cases.

STEP 4. Bake the cupcakes in the preheated oven for
20–25 minutes, until risen and firm to the touch. Transfer
to a wire rack and leave to cool.

STEP 5. Cut a round from the top of each cooled cupcake
with a serrated knife. Sprinkle the cakes with a little cherry
liqueur, if using. Spoon the whipped cream into the
centres and top with a small spoonful of conserve. Gently
replace the tops and dust lightly with cocoa powder.
Store in the refrigerator until ready to serve.

pear & chocolate cupcakes

Makes 12

Difficulty: Medium

Prep: 20 mins, plus cooling
Cook: 20 mins

INGREDIENTS

115 g/4 oz butter, softened

115 g/4 oz light soft
  brown sugar

2 eggs

100 g/3½ oz self-raising flour

½ tsp baking powder

2 tbsp cocoa powder

4 canned pear halves,
  drained and sliced

2 tbsp clear honey, warmed

STEP 1. Preheat the oven to 190°C/375°F/Gas Mark 5. Line a shallow bun tin with 12 paper cases.

STEP 2. Put the butter, sugar, eggs, flour, baking powder and cocoa powder into a mixing bowl and beat until just smooth. Spoon the mixture into the paper cases and smooth the tops. Arrange two pear slices on top of each cupcake.

STEP 3. Bake the cupcakes in the preheated oven for 20 minutes or until risen and just firm to the touch. Transfer to a wire rack. While the cupcakes are still warm, glaze with the honey. Leave to cool completely.

*Note: Make sure that the pears are well drained — if too much syrup is clinging to them it will make the cupcakes soggy.

hot desserts

double chocolate brownies

Makes 9 large or 16 small brownies

Difficulty: Medium

Prep: 25 mins, plus cooling
Cook: 55 mins–1 hour

INGREDIENTS

115 g/4 oz butter, plus extra
   for greasing

115 g/4 oz plain chocolate,
   broken into pieces

300 g/10½ oz golden
   caster sugar

pinch of salt

1 tsp vanilla extract

2 large eggs

140 g/5 oz plain flour

2 tbsp cocoa powder

100 g/3½ oz white chocolate
   chips

FUDGE SAUCE

55 g/2 oz butter

225 g/8 oz golden
   caster sugar

150 ml/5 fl oz milk

250 ml/9 fl oz double cream

225 g/8 oz golden syrup

200 g/7 oz plain chocolate,
   broken into pieces

STEP 1. Preheat the oven to 180°C/350°F/Gas Mark 4. Grease an 18-cm/7-inch square baking tin and line the base with baking paper.

STEP 2. Put the butter and chocolate into a heatproof bowl set over a saucepan of gently simmering water and heat until melted. Stir until smooth. Leave to cool slightly, then stir in the sugar, salt and vanilla extract. Add the eggs, one at a time, and beat until well blended.

STEP 3. Sift the flour and cocoa powder into the mixture and beat until smooth. Stir in the chocolate chips, then pour into the prepared tin. Bake in the preheated oven for 35–40 minutes, or until the top is evenly coloured and a skewer inserted into the centre comes out almost clean. Leave to cool slightly while preparing the sauce.

STEP 4. To make the sauce, put the butter, sugar, milk, cream and golden syrup into a small saucepan over a low heat and stir until the sugar has dissolved. Bring to the boil and stir for 10 minutes, or until the mixture is caramel-coloured. Remove from the heat and add the chocolate. Stir until smooth. Cut the brownies into squares and serve immediately with the sauce.

mochachino brownies with white mocha sauce

Makes 8–10

Difficulty: Medium

Prep: 25 mins, plus cooling
Cook: 40–45 mins

INGREDIENTS

115 g/4 oz butter, plus extra
for greasing

115 g/4 oz plain chocolate

2 tbsp strong black coffee

250 g/9 oz golden
caster sugar

½ tsp ground cinnamon

3 eggs, beaten

85 g/3 oz plain flour

55 g/2 oz milk chocolate
chips

55 g/2 oz toasted walnuts,
skinned and chopped, plus
extra to decorate

WHITE MOCHA SAUCE

100 ml/3½ fl oz double
cream

85 g/3 oz white chocolate

1 tbsp strong black coffee

STEP 1. Preheat the oven to 180°C/350°F/Gas Mark 4. Grease a 23-cm/9-inch square baking tin and line with baking paper.

STEP 2. Put the butter, plain chocolate and coffee into a medium saucepan set over a low heat and stir until just melted and smooth. Leave to cool slightly.

STEP 3. Beat in the sugar, cinnamon and eggs, then beat in the flour, chocolate chips and walnuts. Pour into the prepared tin.

STEP 4. Bake in the preheated oven for 30–35 minutes until just firm but still moist inside. Leave to cool in the tin then cut into squares or bars.

STEP 5. Meanwhile, make the sauce by placing all the ingredients in a small saucepan over a low heat, and stir occasionally until melted and smooth.

STEP 6. Place the brownies on individual plates and spoon the warm sauce on top. Decorate with chopped walnuts and serve.

mint julep brownie cakes

Makes 6–8

Difficulty: Medium

Prep: 25 mins, plus 15 mins cooling
Cook: 40–45 mins

INGREDIENTS

150 g/5½ oz plain chocolate

175 g/6 oz butter, plus extra
  for greasing

2 eggs

200 g/7 oz dark
  muscovado sugar

3 tbsp bourbon

1 tbsp chopped fresh mint

125 g/4½ oz self-raising flour,
  plus extra for dusting

fresh mint sprigs, to decorate

SAUCE

115 g/4 oz plain chocolate

125 ml/4 fl oz single cream

¼ tsp peppermint extract

STEP 1. Preheat the oven to 180°C/350°F/Gas Mark 4. Grease a 28 x 18-cm/11 x 7-inch rectangular baking tin and dust with flour, shaking out any excess.

STEP 2. Put the chocolate and butter into a heatproof bowl set over a saucepan of gently simmering water and heat, stirring occasionally, until melted. Remove from the heat.

STEP 3. Beat together the eggs, sugar, bourbon and chopped mint, then quickly beat into the chocolate mixture. Fold in the flour and mix evenly.

STEP 4. Pour the mixture into the prepared tin and smooth the surface. Bake in the preheated oven for 30–35 minutes until just firm, but still slightly soft inside.

STEP 5. Leave to cool in the tin for 15 minutes, then remove from the tin and use a 7.5-cm/3-inch cutter to stamp out 6–8 rounds.

STEP 6. To make the sauce, put the chocolate, cream and peppermint extract into a small saucepan over a low heat and stir until melted and smooth.

STEP 7. To serve, arrange the brownie cakes on serving plates, drizzle with the warm chocolate sauce and decorate with mint sprigs.

rich ginger brownies with port cream

Makes 8

Difficulty: Medium

Prep: 30 mins, plus cooling
Cook: 40–45 mins

INGREDIENTS

200 g/7 oz plain chocolate

175 g/6 oz butter, plus extra
  for greasing

200 g/7 oz granulated sugar

4 eggs, beaten

2 tsp vanilla extract

1 tbsp stem ginger syrup

100 g/3½ oz plain flour

55 g/2 oz preserved stem
  ginger in syrup, chopped

25 g/1 oz chopped
  crystallized ginger,
  to decorate

PORT CREAM

200 ml/7 fl oz ruby port

200 ml/7 fl oz double cream

1 tbsp icing sugar

1 tsp vanilla extract

STEP 1. Preheat the oven to 180°C/350°F/Gas Mark 4. Grease a 23-cm/9-inch square baking tin.

STEP 2. Put the chocolate and butter into a heatproof bowl set over a saucepan of gently simmering water and heat, stirring, until melted. Remove the bowl from the pan and stir in the sugar.

STEP 3. Beat the eggs, vanilla extract and ginger syrup into the chocolate mixture. Stir in the flour and stem ginger and mix well.

STEP 4. Pour the mixture into the prepared tin and bake in the preheated oven for 30–35 minutes until just firm to the touch.

STEP 5. Meanwhile, make the port cream. Put the port into a saucepan set over a medium-high heat, bring to a simmer and simmer until reduced to about 4 tablespoons. Leave to cool. Whip the cream until beginning to thicken, then add the sugar, port and vanilla extract, whipping until soft peaks hold.

STEP 6. Remove the brownie from the oven, leave to cool in the tin for 2–3 minutes, then cut into eight triangles. Place on individual serving plates and add a spoonful of port cream to each. Top with pieces of crystallized ginger and serve warm.

blonde brownie hearts with raspberry sauce

Makes 8

Difficulty: Medium

Prep: 25 mins, plus 5 mins cooling
Cook: 30–35 mins

INGREDIENTS

115 g/4 oz white chocolate

115 g/4 oz butter, plus extra
for greasing

2 eggs, beaten

150 g/5½ oz caster sugar

seeds from 1 vanilla pod

140 g/5 oz plain flour,
plus extra for dusting

8 small squares plain
chocolate

RASPBERRY SAUCE

250 g/9 oz fresh or frozen
raspberries, thawed if
frozen

2 tbsp amaretto

1 tbsp icing sugar

STEP 1. Preheat the oven to 180°C/350°F/Gas Mark 4.
Grease eight 150-ml/5-fl oz heart-shaped baking tins and
dust with flour, shaking out any excess.

STEP 2. Put the white chocolate and butter into a
heatproof bowl set over a saucepan of gently simmering
water and heat, stirring, until just melted. Remove the
bowl from the pan.

STEP 3. Put the eggs, sugar and vanilla seeds into a
mixing bowl and whisk until smooth and thick. Lightly
fold in the flour, then stir in the chocolate mixture and
mix evenly together. Pour the batter into the prepared tins,
adding a square of plain chocolate to the centre of each,
without pressing down. Bake in the preheated oven for
about 20–25 minutes, or until just firm. Leave to cool in the
tins for 5 minutes.

STEP 4. Meanwhile, make the sauce. Put half the
raspberries, the amaretto and icing sugar into a food
processor and process until smooth. Transfer to a sieve
placed over a bowl and rub through to remove the pips.

STEP 5. Run a knife around the edge of each tin to
loosen, then turn out the hearts onto individual plates.
Spoon the raspberry sauce around the brownies and
decorate with the remaining raspberries. Serve warm.

chocolate blueberry tarts

Makes 10

Difficulty: Medium

Prep: 30 mins, plus chilling and cooling
Cook: 25–30 mins

INGREDIENTS

PASTRY

175 g/6 oz plain flour, plus
  extra for dusting

40 g/1½ oz cocoa powder

55 g/2 oz caster sugar

pinch of salt

125 g/4½ oz butter

1 egg yolk

200 g/7 oz blueberries

2 tbsp crème de cassis

10 g/¼ oz icing sugar, sifted

FILLING

140 g/5 oz plain chocolate,
  broken into pieces

225 ml/8 fl oz double cream

150 ml/5 fl oz soured cream

STEP 1. To make the pastry, put the flour, cocoa powder, sugar and salt into a mixing bowl. Rub in the butter until the mixture resembles breadcrumbs. Add the egg and a little cold water and mix to a dough. Wrap in clingfilm and chill in the refrigerator for 30 minutes.

STEP 2. Preheat the oven to 180°C/350°F/Gas Mark 4. Roll out the pastry on a lightly floured work surface and use to line ten 10-cm/4-inch tartlet tins. Chill in the freezer for 30 minutes, then bake in the preheated oven for 15–20 minutes. Leave to cool.

STEP 3. Put the blueberries, crème de cassis and icing sugar into a saucepan over a low heat and warm through so the berries become shiny, but do not burst. Remove from the heat and leave to cool.

STEP 4. To make the filling, put the chocolate into a heatproof bowl set over a saucepan of gently simmering water and heat until melted, then remove the bowl from the pan and leave to cool slightly. Whip the double cream until it holds stiff peaks, then fold in the soured cream and chocolate.

STEP 5. Turn out the pastry cases onto a serving plate and divide the chocolate filling between them, smoothing the surface, then top with the blueberries.

hot chocolate soufflés with coffee sabayon

Serves 6

Difficulty: Hard

Prep: 30 mins, plus cooling
Cook: 40–45 mins

INGREDIENTS

butter, for greasing

3 tbsp cornflour

250 ml/9 fl oz milk

115 g/4 oz plain chocolate,
 broken into pieces

4 eggs, separated

55 g/2 oz golden caster
 sugar, plus extra for coating

icing sugar, for dusting

COFFEE SABAYON

2 eggs

3 egg yolks

85 g/3 oz golden
 caster sugar

4 tsp instant coffee granules

2 tbsp brandy

STEP 1. Preheat the oven to 190°C/375°F/Gas Mark 5. Grease six medium-sized ramekins with butter and coat with caster sugar. Put the cornflour into a mixing bowl. Add a little milk and stir until smooth. Pour the remaining milk into a heavy-based saucepan and add the chocolate. Heat over a low heat until the chocolate has melted, then stir. Pour the chocolate milk onto the cornflour paste, stirring. Return to the pan, increase the heat to medium and bring to the boil, stirring. Reduce the heat and simmer for 1 minute. Remove from the heat and stir in the egg yolks, one at a time. Cover and cool slightly.

STEP 2. Put the egg whites into a clean, greasefree bowl and whisk until soft peaks hold. Gradually whisk in the caster sugar until stiff but not dry. Stir a little of the meringue into the chocolate mixture, then carefully fold in the remainder. Pour into the prepared ramekins and bake in the preheated oven for 25–30 minutes, or until well risen and slightly wobbly when pushed.

STEP 3. Just before the soufflés are ready, make the coffee sabayon. Put all the ingredients into a heavy-based saucepan over a very low heat and whisk constantly until the mixture is thick and light. Dust a little icing sugar over the soufflés and serve immediately with the sabayon.

individual chocolate fondant puddings

Serves 4

Difficulty: Medium

Prep: 20 mins, plus cooling and 1 minute standing
Cook: 17–20 mins

INGREDIENTS

100 g/3½ oz butter, plus
 extra for greasing

100 g/3½ oz plain chocolate,
 broken into pieces

2 eggs

1 tsp vanilla extract

100 g/3½ oz golden
 caster sugar, plus extra
 for sprinkling

2 tbsp plain flour

sifted icing sugar, for dusting

lightly whipped cream,
 to serve

STEP 1. Preheat the oven to 200°C/400°F/Gas Mark 6. Grease four 175-ml/6-fl oz pudding basins or ramekins with butter and sprinkle with caster sugar.

STEP 2. Put the butter and chocolate into a heatproof bowl set over a saucepan of gently simmering water and heat until melted. Stir until smooth, then remove the bowl from the pan and leave to cool.

STEP 3. Put the eggs, vanilla extract, caster sugar and flour into a mixing bowl and whisk together. Stir in the melted chocolate mixture. Pour into the prepared pudding basins and place on a baking tray. Bake in the preheated oven for 12–15 minutes, or until the puddings are well risen and set on the outside but still molten inside.

STEP 4. Leave to stand for 1 minute, then turn out the puddings onto serving plates. Dust with icing sugar and serve immediately with whipped cream.

chocolate orange pots

Serves 4

Difficulty: Easy

Prep: 20 mins
Cook: 5 mins

INGREDIENTS

1 orange

125 g/4½ oz plain chocolate,
  broken into pieces

30 g/1 oz butter

3 tbsp maple syrup

1 tbsp orange liqueur

125 g/4½ oz crème fraîche

strips of orange zest,
  to decorate

STEP 1. Cut the white pith and peel from the orange and lift out the segments, catching the juice in a bowl. Cut the segments into small chunks.

STEP 2. Put the chocolate, butter, maple syrup, liqueur and reserved orange juice into a small saucepan and heat very gently, stirring, until smooth.

STEP 3. Stir in 4 tablespoons of the crème fraîche and the orange chunks.

STEP 4. Spoon the mixture into serving dishes, then top each with a spoonful of the remaining crème fraîche.

STEP 5. Scatter strips of orange zest over the top and serve warm.

*Note: This elegant dessert is also extremely rich, so serve it after a light meal if you want it to be properly appreciated.

pear & hazelnut pancakes

Serves 4

Difficulty: Easy

Prep: 20 mins
Cook: 10 mins

INGREDIENTS

200 g/7 oz chocolate
  hazelnut spread

8 ready-made pancakes

4 ripe pears, peeled,
  cored and chopped

40 g/1½ oz butter, melted

2 tbsp demerara sugar

55 g/2 oz toasted chopped
  hazelnuts, to serve

STEP 1. Preheat the grill to high. Put the chocolate hazelnut spread into a small saucepan set over a low heat and heat until soft.

STEP 2. Using a palette knife, spread each pancake with a little of the warmed chocolate spread.

STEP 3. Arrange the pears over the chocolate spread, then bring the opposite sides of the pancakes over the filling to enclose it.

STEP 4. Lightly brush an ovenproof dish with a little of the melted butter.

STEP 5. Arrange the pancakes in the dish. Brush the pancakes with the remaining melted butter and sprinkle with the sugar.

STEP 6. Place the dish under the preheated grill and cook for 4–5 minutes until bubbling and lightly browned.

STEP 7. Scatter the toasted hazelnuts over the pancakes and serve hot.

chocolate filo parcels

Makes 18

Difficulty: Easy

Prep: 20 mins
Cook: 10 mins

INGREDIENTS

85 g/3 oz ground hazelnuts

1 tbsp finely chopped fresh
  mint

125 ml/4 fl oz soured cream

2 eating apples, peeled and
  grated

55 g/2 oz plain chocolate,
  melted

9 sheets filo pastry, about
  15 cm/6 inches square

55–85 g/2–3 oz butter,
  melted, plus extra for
  greasing

sifted icing sugar, for dusting

STEP 1. Preheat the oven to 190°C/375°F/Gas Mark 5.
Grease a baking tray.

STEP 2. Put the nuts, mint and soured cream into a mixing
bowl and mix to combine. Add the apples, stir in the
chocolate and mix well.

STEP 3. Cut each pastry sheet into four squares. Brush
one square with butter, then place a second square on
top and brush with butter.

STEP 4. Place a tablespoon of the chocolate mixture in
the centre of the pastry square, then bring up the corners
and twist together. Repeat until all of the pastry and
filling have been used.

STEP 5. Place the parcels on the prepared tray
and bake in the preheated oven for about 10 minutes
until crisp and golden. Remove from the oven and leave
to cool slightly. Dust with icing sugar and serve.

chocolate apple lattice tart

Serves 6

Difficulty: Medium

Prep: 30 mins, plus 45 mins chilling, and cooling
Cook: 40–45 mins

INGREDIENTS

200 g/7 oz plain flour,
 plus extra for dusting

2 tbsp cocoa powder

3 tbsp caster sugar

100 g/3½ oz butter, diced,
 plus extra for greasing

1–2 egg yolks, beaten

FILLING

225 g/8 oz double cream

2 eggs, beaten

1 tsp ground cinnamon

115 g/4 oz plain chocolate,
 grated

4 eating apples, peeled,
 sliced and brushed with
 lemon juice

3 tbsp demerara sugar

STEP 1. Sift the flour and cocoa powder into a mixing bowl. Stir in the caster sugar, then add the butter and rub in with your fingertips until the mixture resembles fine breadcrumbs. Stir in enough egg yolk to mix to a dough. Shape into a ball, wrap in foil and chill in the refrigerator for 45 minutes.

STEP 2. Preheat the oven to 180°C/350°F/Gas Mark 4. Grease a 20-cm/8-inch loose-based round tart tin. Roll out the dough on a lightly floured work surface and use three quarters of it to line the tin.

STEP 3. To make the filling, beat together the cream, eggs (reserving a little for glazing), cinnamon and chocolate. Put the apples into a bowl, pour over the cream mixture and stir. Spoon the mixture into the tart tin, then sprinkle over the demerara sugar.

STEP 4. Roll out the remaining dough and cut into long strips, then arrange over the tart in a lattice pattern. Brush the pastry strips with the reserved egg, then bake in the preheated oven for 40–45 minutes.

STEP 5. Remove from the oven and leave in the tin to cool to room temperature before serving.

pear tart with chocolate sauce

Serves 6

Difficulty: Medium

Prep: 35 mins, plus chilling and cooling
Cook: 40 mins

INGREDIENTS

100 g/3½ oz plain flour

25 g/1 oz ground almonds

60 g/2¼ oz butter, plus extra
for greasing

about 3 tbsp water

FILLING

50 g/1¾ oz butter

50 g/1¾ oz caster sugar

2 eggs, beaten

100 g/3½ oz ground almonds

2 tbsp cocoa powder

a few drops of almond
extract

400 g/14 oz canned pear
halves in natural juice,
drained

CHOCOLATE SAUCE

4 tbsp caster sugar

3 tbsp golden syrup

100 ml/3½ fl oz water

175 g/6 oz plain chocolate,
broken into pieces

25 g/1 oz butter

STEP 1. Preheat the oven to 200°C/400°F/Gas Mark 6. Lightly grease a 20-cm/8-inch round tart tin.

STEP 2. Sift the flour into a mixing bowl and stir in the ground almonds. Rub in the butter with your fingertips until the mixture resembles breadcrumbs. Add enough water to mix to a soft dough. Cover and chill in the freezer for 10 minutes, then roll out and use to line the prepared tin. Prick the base with a fork and chill again.

STEP 3. To make the filling, put the butter and sugar into a mixing bowl and cream together until light and fluffy. Beat in the eggs, then fold in the ground almonds, cocoa powder and almond extract. Spread the mixture over the base of the pastry case. Thinly slice each pear widthways, flatten slightly, then arrange the slices on top of the chocolate mixture, pressing down lightly. Bake in the preheated oven for 30 minutes, or until the filling has risen. Leave to cool slightly in the tin, then transfer to a serving plate.

STEP 4. To make the chocolate sauce, put the sugar, golden syrup and water into a saucepan over a low heat and stir until the sugar dissolves. Increase the heat, bring to the boil and boil gently for 1 minute. Remove from the heat, add the chocolate and butter and stir until melted and well combined. Serve with the tart.

chocolate pecan pie

Serves 6–8

Difficulty: Medium

Prep: 20 mins, plus 1½ hours chilling, and cooling
Cook: 45–50 mins

INGREDIENTS

175 g/6 oz plain flour,
   plus extra for dusting

100 g/3½ oz butter

1 tbsp golden caster sugar

1 egg yolk,
   beaten with 1 tbsp water

FILLING

55 g/2 oz butter

3 tbsp cocoa powder

225 ml/8 fl oz golden syrup

3 eggs

70 g/2½ oz soft dark
   brown sugar

175 g/6 oz pecan nuts

STEP 1. Sift the flour into a mixing bowl. Rub in the butter with your fingertips until the mixture resembles breadcrumbs. Stir in the sugar, then add the beaten egg yolk. Lightly knead to a firm dough. Cover and chill in the refrigerator for 1½ hours.

STEP 2. Preheat the oven to 190°C/375°F/Gas Mark 5. Roll out the pastry on a lightly floured surface and use to line a 20-cm/8-inch round tart tin. Put a baking sheet in the oven to heat.

STEP 3. To make the filling, put the butter into a saucepan and heat over a low heat until melted. Sift in the cocoa powder and stir in the golden syrup. Put the eggs and sugar into a bowl and beat together. Stir in the butter mixture and the pecan nuts.

STEP 4. Pour the mixture into the pastry case, place on the preheated baking tray and bake for 35–40 minutes until just set. Leave to cool slightly and serve warm.

chocolate meringue pie

Serves 6

Difficulty: Hard

Prep: 35 mins
Cook: 50 mins

INGREDIENTS

55 g/2 oz butter, melted

225 g/8 oz plain chocolate
  digestive biscuits, crushed

FILLING

3 egg yolks

4 tbsp caster sugar

4 tbsp cornflour

600 ml/1 pint milk

100 g/3½ oz plain chocolate,
  broken into pieces

MERINGUE

2 egg whites

100 g/3½ oz caster sugar

½ tsp vanilla extract

STEP 1. Preheat the oven to 190°C/375°F/Gas Mark 5. Put the butter into a bowl, add the crushed biscuits and stir until well combined. Press the mixture firmly into the base and up the side of a 23-cm/9-inch round tart tin.

STEP 2. To make the filling, put the egg yolks, sugar and cornflour into a mixing bowl and beat until a smooth paste forms. Put the milk into a heavy-based saucepan and heat until almost boiling, then slowly pour it onto the egg mixture, whisking well.

STEP 3. Return the mixture to the pan and cook over a low heat, whisking until it thickens. Remove from the heat. Put the chocolate into a heatproof bowl set over a saucepan of gently simmering water and heat until melted. Whisk into the egg mixture and pour into the biscuit base.

STEP 4. To make the meringue, put the egg whites into a large mixing bowl and whisk until soft peaks hold. Gradually whisk in about two thirds of the sugar until the mixture is stiff and glossy. Fold in the remaining sugar and the vanilla extract.

STEP 5. Spread the meringue over the chocolate filling, swirling the surface with the back of a spoon to give it an attractive finish. Bake in the centre of the preheated oven for 30 minutes, or until the meringue is golden. Serve the pie hot or just warm.

hot chocolate cheesecake

Serves 8–10

Difficulty: Medium

Prep: 35 mins, plus 30 mins chilling
Cook: 1½ hours

INGREDIENTS

150 g/5½ oz plain flour, plus
  extra for dusting

2 tbsp cocoa powder

55 g/2 oz butter, plus extra
  for greasing

2 tbsp golden caster sugar

25 g/1 oz ground almonds

1 egg yolk

FILLING

2 eggs, separated

75 g/2¾ oz golden
  caster sugar

350 g/12 oz cream cheese

4 tbsp ground almonds

150 ml/5 fl oz double cream

25 g/1 oz cocoa powder,
  sifted

1 tsp vanilla extract

sifted icing sugar, for dusting

grated milk chocolate,
  to decorate

STEP 1. Grease a 20-cm/8-inch round loose-based cake tin. Sift the flour and cocoa powder into a mixing bowl and rub in the butter with your fingertips until the mixture resembles fine breadcrumbs. Stir in the sugar and ground almonds. Add the egg yolk and enough water to mix to a soft dough.

STEP 2. Roll out the pastry on a lightly floured work surface and use to line the prepared tin. Chill in the refrigerator for 30 minutes. Preheat the oven to 160°C/325°F/Gas Mark 3.

STEP 3. To make the filling, put the egg yolks and caster sugar into a mixing bowl and whisk until thick and pale. Beat in the cream cheese, ground almonds, cream, cocoa powder and vanilla extract until well combined.

STEP 4. Put the egg whites into a clean, greasefree bowl and whisk until stiff but not dry. Stir a little of the egg whites into the cheese mixture, then fold in the remainder. Pour into the pastry case.

STEP 5. Bake in the preheated oven for 1½ hours, or until well risen and just firm to the touch. Carefully remove from the tin, dust with icing sugar and sprinkle with grated chocolate. Serve warm.

chocolate fruit crumble

Serves 4

Difficulty: Easy

Prep: 25 mins
Cook: 40–45 mins

INGREDIENTS

butter, for greasing

400 g/14 oz canned apricots
in natural juice

450 g/1 lb cooking apples,
peeled and thickly sliced

CRUMBLE TOPPING

100 g/3½ oz plain flour

85 g/3 oz butter

50 g/1¾ oz porridge oats

4 tbsp caster sugar

55 g/2 oz plain chocolate
chips or milk
chocolate chips

single cream or double
cream, to serve

STEP 1. Preheat the oven to 180°C/350°F/Gas Mark 4. Lightly grease an ovenproof dish.

STEP 2. Drain the apricots, reserving 4 tablespoons of the juice. Put the apples and apricots into the prepared dish with the reserved apricot juice and toss to mix.

STEP 3. To make the crumble topping, sift the flour into a mixing bowl and rub in the butter with your fingertips until the mixture resembles fine breadcrumbs. Stir in the porridge oats, sugar and chocolate chips.

STEP 4. Sprinkle the crumble mixture over the apples and apricots and smooth the top lightly. Do not press the crumble into the fruit.

STEP 5. Bake in the preheated oven for 40–45 minutes, or until the topping is golden. Serve hot with cream.

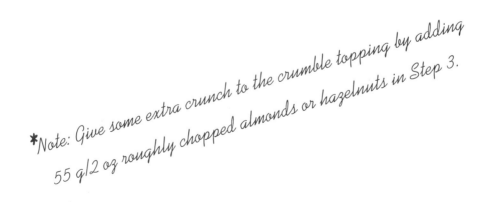

*Note: Give some extra crunch to the crumble topping by adding 55 g/2 oz roughly chopped almonds or hazelnuts in Step 3.

profiteroles & chocolate sauce

Serves 4

Difficulty: Hard

Prep: 25 mins, plus cooling
Cook: 40 mins

INGREDIENTS

CHOUX PASTRY

200 ml/7 fl oz water

70 g/2½ oz butter, plus extra
for greasing

100 g/3½ oz plain flour, sifted

3 eggs, beaten

CREAM FILLING

300 ml/10 fl oz double cream

3 tbsp caster sugar

1 tsp vanilla extract

CHOCOLATE SAUCE

125 g/4½ oz plain chocolate,
broken into small pieces

35 g/1¼ oz butter

6 tbsp water

2 tbsp brandy

STEP 1. Preheat the oven to 200°C/400°F/Gas Mark 6. Grease a large baking tray.

STEP 2. To make the choux pastry, put the water and butter into a saucepan and bring to the boil. Immediately add all the flour, remove the pan from the heat and stir the mixture into a paste that leaves the side of the pan clean. Leave to cool slightly. Beat in enough of the eggs to give the mixture a soft dropping consistency.

STEP 3. Spoon the mixture into a piping bag fitted with a 1-cm/½-inch plain nozzle. Pipe small balls onto the prepared tray and bake in the preheated oven for 25 minutes. Remove from the oven. Pierce each ball with a skewer to allow the steam to escape.

STEP 4. To make the filling, whip together the cream, sugar and vanilla extract. Cut the pastry balls almost in half, then fill with cream.

STEP 5. To make the sauce, put the chocolate, butter and water into a heatproof bowl set over a saucepan of gently simmering water and stir until smooth. Stir in the brandy. Pile the profiteroles into individual serving dishes or into a pyramid on a raised cake stand. Drizzle the sauce over the profiteroles and serve warm.

chocolate fondue

Serves 6

Difficulty: Easy

Prep: 30 mins, plus chilling
Cook: 5 mins

INGREDIENTS

1 pineapple

1 mango

12 Cape gooseberries

250 g/9 oz fresh strawberries

250 g/9 oz seedless green
  grapes

FONDUE

250 g/9 oz plain chocolate,
  broken into pieces

150 ml/5 fl oz double cream

2 tbsp brandy

STEP 1. Using a sharp knife, peel and core the pineapple, then cut the flesh into cubes. Peel and stone the mango and cut the flesh into cubes. Peel back the papery outer skin of the Cape gooseberries and twist at the top to make a 'handle'. Arrange all the fruit on six serving plates and chill in the refrigerator.

STEP 2. To make the fondue, put the chocolate and cream into a fondue pot. Heat gently, stirring constantly, until the chocolate has melted. Stir in the brandy until thoroughly blended and the chocolate mixture is smooth.

STEP 3. Place the fondue pot over the burner to keep warm. To serve, allow each guest to dip the fruit into the sauce, using fondue forks or bamboo skewers.

chocolate zabaglione

Serves 4

Difficulty: Medium

Prep: 15 mins
Cook: 15 mins

INGREDIENTS

4 egg yolks

4 tbsp caster sugar

50 g/1¾ oz plain chocolate

125 ml/4 fl oz Marsala

cocoa powder, for dusting

STEP 1. Put the egg yolks and sugar into a large heatproof bowl and beat with a hand-held electric mixer until very pale.

STEP 2. Finely grate the chocolate and fold into the egg mixture. Fold in the Marsala.

STEP 3. Set the bowl over a saucepan of gently simmering water and set the electric mixer to the lowest speed or swap to a balloon whisk. Cook gently, whisking constantly, until the mixture thickens. Do not overcook or the mixture will curdle.

STEP 4. Spoon the hot mixture into four heatproof glasses and dust with cocoa powder. Serve warm.

*Note: You must keep beating the zabaglione as it cooks, otherwise not enough air will be introduced and it will not have its characteristic lightness. For added texture, replace the cocoa powder with 25 g/1 oz crushed amaretti biscuits.

cool
desserts

rich chocolate mousses

Makes 4

Difficulty: Medium

Prep: 20 mins, plus cooling and 4 hours chilling
Cook: 5 mins

INGREDIENTS

300 g/10½ oz plain
  chocolate, broken into
  pieces

5 tbsp caster sugar

1½ tbsp butter

1 tbsp brandy

4 eggs, separated

cocoa powder, for dusting

STEP 1. Put the chocolate into a heatproof bowl set over a saucepan of gently simmering water. Add the sugar and butter and stir until smooth. Remove the bowl from the pan, stir in the brandy, and leave to cool slightly. Add the egg yolks and beat until smooth.

STEP 2. Put the egg whites into a clean, greasefree bowl, whisk until stiff peaks hold, then fold them into the chocolate mixture. Place a stainless steel cooking ring on each of four small serving plates, then spoon the mixture into the rings and smooth the surfaces. Chill in the refrigerator for at least 4 hours until set.

STEP 3. Take the mousses out of the refrigerator and carefully remove the cooking rings. Dust with cocoa powder and serve immediately.

brown sugar mocha cream dessert

Serves 4

Difficulty: Easy

Prep: 20 mins, plus chilling
Cook: None

INGREDIENTS

300 ml/10 fl oz double cream

1 tsp vanilla extract

85 g/3 oz fresh wholemeal
  breadcrumbs

85 g/3 oz dark brown sugar

1 tbsp instant
  coffee granules

2 tbsp cocoa powder

grated milk chocolate, to
  decorate

STEP 1. Put the cream and vanilla extract into a large bowl and whip until thick and soft peaks hold.

STEP 2. Put the breadcrumbs, sugar, coffee granules and cocoa powder into a separate bowl and mix together.

STEP 3. Layer the breadcrumb mixture with the whipped cream in serving glasses, finishing with a layer of whipped cream. Sprinkle with the grated chocolate.

STEP 4. Cover with clingfilm and chill in the refrigerator for several hours, or overnight.

STEP 5. Remove from the refrigerator and serve.

*Note: This creamy, make-ahead dessert will add a wow factor to your dinner parties. You can give it an extra touch of indulgence and a deeper coffee flavour by adding 1–2 tablespoons of coffee liqueur with the vanilla extract in Step 1.

white chocolate tiramisù

Serves 4

Difficulty: Easy

Prep: 20 mins, plus 2 hours chilling
Cook: None

INGREDIENTS

16 Italian sponge fingers

250 ml/9 fl oz strong black coffee, cooled to room temperature

4 tbsp almond-flavoured liqueur, such as amaretto

250 g/9 oz mascarpone cheese

300 ml/10 fl oz double cream

3 tbsp caster sugar

125 g/4½ oz white chocolate, grated

4 tbsp toasted flaked almonds, to decorate

STEP 1. Break the sponge fingers into pieces and divide half of them between four serving glasses. Mix the coffee and liqueur together in a jug, then pour half over the sponge fingers in the glasses.

STEP 2. Put the mascarpone cheese, cream, sugar and 50 g/1¾ oz of the chocolate into a mixing bowl and beat together. Spread half the mixture over the coffee-soaked sponge fingers, then arrange the remaining sponge fingers on top. Pour over the remaining coffee mixture, then spread over the remaining cream mixture. Sprinkle with the remaining chocolate.

STEP 3. Cover with clingfilm and chill for at least 2 hours, or until required. Sprinkle over the flaked almonds just before serving.

chocolate ice cream bites

Serves 6

Difficulty: Easy

Prep: 15 mins, plus chilling
Cook: 5 mins

INGREDIENTS

600 g/1 lb 5 oz vanilla
  ice cream

200 g/7 oz plain chocolate

2 tbsp butter

STEP 1. Line a baking tray with clingfilm.

STEP 2. Cut the ice cream into bite-sized cubes and place them on the prepared tray. Stick a cocktail stick in each piece and freeze until very hard.

STEP 3. Put the chocolate and butter into a heatproof bowl set over a saucepan of gently simmering water and heat until melted. Quickly dip the frozen ice cream cubes into the warm chocolate mixture and return them to the freezer until ready to serve.

*Note: You can vary the flavour of the ice cream to taste — why not try peach, pistachio or rum & raisin? Or reverse the appearance of the bites and dip chocolate ice cream cubes in melted white chocolate couverture.

chocolate banana sundae

Serves 4

Difficulty: Easy

Prep: 20 mins
Cook: 5 mins

INGREDIENTS

150 ml/5 fl oz double cream

4 bananas, peeled

8 scoops good-quality vanilla
  ice cream

75 g/2¾ oz chopped mixed
  nuts, toasted

grated milk chocolate
  or plain chocolate, for
  sprinkling

4 fan wafers, to serve

CHOCOLATE SAUCE

55 g/2 oz plain chocolate,
  broken into pieces

4 tbsp golden syrup

15 g/½ oz butter

1 tbsp brandy or dark rum
  (optional)

STEP 1. To make the chocolate sauce, put the chocolate, golden syrup and butter into a heatproof bowl set over a saucepan of gently simmering water and stir until melted and well combined. Remove the bowl from the pan and stir in the brandy, if using.

STEP 2. Whip the cream until it just holds its shape. Slice the bananas. Place a scoop of ice cream in the base of four sundae glasses. Top with slices of banana, some chocolate sauce, a spoonful of cream and a generous sprinkling of nuts.

STEP 3. Repeat the layers, finishing with a good dollop of cream, then sprinkle with the remaining nuts and the grated chocolate. Add a wafer to each glass and serve.

chocolate hazelnut pots

Serves 4

Difficulty: Medium

Prep: 20 mins, plus cooling and chilling
Cook: 50–55 mins

INGREDIENTS

2 eggs

2 egg yolks

1 tbsp caster sugar

1 tsp cornflour

600 ml/1 pint milk

85 g/3 oz plain chocolate

4 tbsp chocolate
   hazelnut spread

lightly whipped cream and
   chocolate caraque,
   to decorate

STEP 1. Preheat the oven to 160°C/325°F/Gas Mark 3.

STEP 2. Put the eggs, egg yolks, sugar and cornflour into a mixing bowl and beat together until well combined. Heat the milk in a small saucepan until it is almost boiling. Gradually pour the milk onto the eggs, whisking constantly. Put the chocolate and chocolate hazelnut spread into a heatproof bowl set over a saucepan of gently simmering water and heat until melted, then whisk into the egg mixture.

STEP 3. Pour into four small ovenproof dishes and cover the dishes with foil. Place them in a roasting tin. Fill the tin with boiling water until it comes halfway up the sides of the dishes. Bake in the preheated oven for 35–40 minutes until the custard is just set.

STEP 4. Remove from the tin and leave to cool, then chill until required. Serve decorated with whipped cream and chocolate caraque.

chocolate rum pots

Makes 6

Difficulty: Medium

Prep: 20 mins, plus cooling and 2 hours chilling
Cook: 5 mins

INGREDIENTS

225 g/8 oz plain chocolate

4 eggs, separated

6 tbsp caster sugar

4 tbsp dark rum

4 tbsp double cream

whipped cream and marbled
  chocolate shapes, to
  decorate

STEP 1. Put the chocolate into a heatproof bowl set over a saucepan of gently simmering water and heat until melted. Remove the bowl from the pan and leave to cool slightly.

STEP 2. Put the egg yolks and sugar into a separate bowl and whisk together until very pale and fluffy.

STEP 3. Drizzle the melted chocolate into the egg mixture and fold in with the rum and double cream.

STEP 4. Put the egg whites into a clean, greasefree bowl and whisk until soft peaks hold. Fold into the chocolate mixture in two batches. Divide between six serving dishes and chill in the refrigerator for at least 2 hours.

STEP 5. To serve, decorate with a little whipped cream and top with marbled chocolate shapes.

*Note: The rum makes this dessert very aromatic — if you don't like rum, replace it with brandy or coffee liqueur.

chocolate & vanilla creams

Makes 4

Difficulty: Medium

Prep: 20 mins, plus 15–20 mins chilling
Cook: 10–15 mins

INGREDIENTS

450 ml/16 fl oz double cream

6 tbsp caster sugar

1 vanilla pod

200 ml/7 fl oz crème fraîche

3 tbsp water

2 tsp powdered gelatine

50 g/1¾ oz plain chocolate,
  broken into pieces

chopped marbled chocolate
  caraque, to decorate

STEP 1. Put the cream and sugar into a saucepan with the vanilla pod. Heat gently, stirring, until the sugar has dissolved, then bring to the boil. Reduce the heat and simmer for 2–3 minutes.

STEP 2. Remove from the heat and take out the vanilla pod. Stir in the crème fraîche.

STEP 3. Put the water into a small heatproof bowl and sprinkle over the gelatine. Leave to stand until spongy, then set over a saucepan of hot water and stir until dissolved. Stir into the cream mixture. Pour half of this mixture into a separate mixing bowl.

STEP 4. Put the chocolate into a heatproof bowl set over a saucepan of gently simmering water and heat until melted. Stir the melted chocolate into half of the cream mixture. Pour the chocolate mixture into four individual glasses and chill for 15–20 minutes until just set. Keep the vanilla mixture at room temperature.

STEP 5. Spoon the vanilla mixture on top of the chocolate mixture and chill until set. When ready to serve, decorate with the chopped caraque.

chocolate meringues

Makes 8

Difficulty: Hard

Prep: 30 mins, plus cooling and setting
Cook: 1 hour 5 mins

INGREDIENTS

4 egg whites

200 g/7 oz caster sugar

1 tsp cornflour

40 g/1½ oz plain chocolate, grated

FILLING

100 g/3½ oz plain chocolate

150 ml/5 fl oz double cream

1 tbsp icing sugar

1 tbsp brandy (optional)

STEP 1. Preheat the oven to 140°C/275°F/Gas Mark 1. Line two baking trays with baking paper.

STEP 2. Put the egg whites into a clean, greasefree bowl and whisk until soft peaks hold, then gradually whisk in half the caster sugar. Continue whisking until the mixture is very stiff and glossy.

STEP 3. Carefully fold in the remaining caster sugar, the cornflour and grated chocolate with a metal spoon or palette knife. Spoon the mixture into a piping bag fitted with a large star nozzle or plain nozzle. Pipe 16 large rosettes or mounds onto the prepared trays.

STEP 4. Bake in the preheated oven for about 1 hour, turning the trays after 30 minutes. Without opening the oven door, switch off the oven and leave the meringues to cool inside. Remove from the oven and carefully peel off the baking paper.

STEP 5. To make the filling, put the chocolate into a heatproof bowl set over a saucepan of gently simmering water and heat until melted. Carefully spread it over the bases of the meringues. Stand them upside down on a wire rack until the chocolate has set. Whip the cream with the icing sugar and brandy, if using, until it holds its shape, then use to sandwich the chocolate-coated meringues together in pairs.

chocolate trifle

Serves 8

Difficulty: Medium

Prep: 25 mins, plus cooling and chilling
Cook: 15 mins

INGREDIENTS

280 g/10 oz ready-made
  chocolate loaf cake

3–4 tbsp seedless
  raspberry jam

4 tbsp amaretto

250 g/9 oz frozen mixed
  berries, thawed

chocolate truffles and
  chocolate shapes,
  to decorate

CHOCOLATE CUSTARD

6 egg yolks

55 g/2 oz caster sugar

1 tbsp cornflour

500 ml/18 fl oz milk

55 g/2 oz plain chocolate,
  broken into pieces

TOPPING

225 ml/8 fl oz double cream

1 tbsp caster sugar

½ tsp vanilla extract

STEP 1. Cut the cake into slices and make 'sandwiches' with the raspberry jam. Cut the 'sandwiches' into cubes and place in a large glass serving bowl. Sprinkle with the amaretto. Spread the berries over the cake.

STEP 2. To make the custard, put the egg yolks and sugar into a bowl and whisk until thick and pale. Stir in the cornflour. Put the milk into a saucepan and heat until almost boiling. Pour into the egg yolk mixture, stirring. Return the mixture to the pan and bring just to the boil, stirring constantly, until it thickens. Remove from the heat and leave to cool slightly.

STEP 3. Put the chocolate into a heatproof bowl set over a saucepan of gently simmering water and heat until melted, then add to the custard. Pour the custard over the cake and berries. Cool, cover and chill for 2 hours, or until set.

STEP 4. To make the topping, put the cream into a bowl and whip until soft peaks hold. Beat in the sugar and vanilla extract. Spoon over the trifle. Decorate with chocolate truffles and chocolate shapes and chill until ready to serve.

white truffle cake

Serves 12

Difficulty: Medium

Prep: 30 mins, plus cooling and 2 hours chilling
Cook: 40 mins

INGREDIENTS

butter, for greasing

50 g/1¾ oz white chocolate

2 eggs

50 g/1¾ oz caster sugar

70 g/2½ oz plain flour, sifted

TRUFFLE TOPPING

300 ml/10 fl oz double cream

350 g/12 oz white chocolate,
  broken into pieces

250 g/9 oz mascarpone
  cheese

50 g/1¾ oz white chocolate
  shavings

STEP 1. Preheat the oven to 180°C/ 350°F/Gas Mark 4. Grease a 20-cm/8-inch round springform cake tin and line the base with baking paper.

STEP 2. Put the chocolate into a heatproof bowl set over a saucepan of gently simmering water and heat until melted.

STEP 3. Put the eggs and sugar into a mixing bowl and beat with a hand-held electric mixer until thick and pale – the mixture should leave a trail when the whisk is lifted. Gently fold the flour into the egg mixture with a metal spoon. Add the melted chocolate.

STEP 4. Pour the mixture into the prepared tin and bake in the preheated oven for 25 minutes, or until springy to the touch. Leave to cool slightly in the tin, then transfer to a wire rack and leave to cool completely. Return the cooled cake to the tin.

STEP 5. To make the topping, put the cream into a saucepan and bring to the boil, stirring constantly. Remove from the heat and leave to cool slightly, then return to the heat, add the chocolate pieces and stir until melted and combined. Remove from the heat and stir until almost cool, then mix in the mascarpone cheese.

STEP 6. Pour the topping over the cake and chill in the refrigerator for 2 hours. Decorate with the chocolate shavings before serving.

citrus cake

Serves 12

Difficulty: Medium

Prep: 30 mins, plus cooling and chilling
Cook: 45 mins

INGREDIENTS

175 g/6 oz butter, plus extra
   for greasing

175 g/6 oz caster sugar

4 eggs, beaten

200 g/7 oz self-raising flour

1 tbsp cocoa powder

50 g/1¾ oz orange-flavoured
   plain chocolate, melted

peeled orange segments,
   to decorate

ORANGE MOUSSE

2 eggs, separated

50 g/1¾ oz caster sugar

200 ml/7 fl oz freshly
   squeezed orange juice

2 tsp gelatine

3 tbsp water

300 ml/10 fl oz double cream

STEP 1. Preheat the oven to 180°C/350°F/Gas Mark 4. Grease a 20-cm/8-inch round cake tin and line the base with baking paper. Put the butter and sugar in a mixing bowl and cream together until light and fluffy. Gradually add the eggs, beating well after each addition. Sift in the flour and cocoa powder and fold into the creamed mixture. Fold in the melted chocolate. Pour into the prepared tin and level the top. Bake in the preheated oven for 40 minutes, or until springy to the touch. Leave to cool for 5 minutes in the tin, then turn out onto a wire rack and leave to cool completely. Cut the cold cake horizontally into two layers.

STEP 2. To make the orange mousse, put the egg yolks and sugar into a mixing bowl and beat until pale, then beat in the orange juice. Put the water into a small heatproof bowl, sprinkle over the gelatine and leave until spongy, then place over a saucepan of hot water and stir until dissolved. Stir into the egg yolk mixture. Whip the cream until it holds its shape. Reserve a little for decoration, then fold the remainder into the orange mixture. Put the egg whites into a clean, greasefree bowl and whisk until soft peaks hold, then fold into the orange mixture. Leave to stand in a cool place until starting to set, stirring occasionally.

STEP 3. Return one cake layer to the tin. Pour in the mousse and press the second cake layer on top. Chill until set. Transfer to a serving plate, spoon teaspoons of cream around the top and decorate with orange segments.

crispy chocolate pie

Serves 6

Difficulty: Medium

Prep: 30 mins, plus cooling
Cook: 40–45 mins

INGREDIENTS

butter, for greasing

2 egg whites

100 g/3½ oz ground almonds

4 tbsp ground rice

125 g/4½ oz caster sugar

¼ tsp almond extract

225 g/8 oz plain chocolate,
  broken into small pieces

4 egg yolks

4 tbsp icing sugar

4 tbsp whisky

4 tbsp double cream

TO DECORATE

150 ml/5 fl oz whipped cream

marbled chocolate caraque

STEP 1. Preheat the oven to 160°C/325°F/Gas Mark 3. Grease a 20-cm/8-inch flan tin and line the base with baking paper. Put the egg whites into a clean, greasefree bowl and whisk until stiff peaks hold. Gently fold in the ground almonds, ground rice, caster sugar and almond extract. Spread the mixture over the base and side of the prepared tin. Bake in the preheated oven for 15 minutes.

STEP 2. Meanwhile, put the chocolate into a heatproof bowl set over a saucepan of gently simmering water and heat until melted. Remove the bowl from the pan and leave to cool slightly, then beat in the egg yolks, icing sugar, whisky and double cream until thoroughly incorporated.

STEP 3. Remove the tin from the oven and pour in the chocolate mixture. Cover with foil, return to the oven and bake for 20–25 minutes until set. Remove from the oven and leave in the tin to cool completely.

STEP 4. Turn out of the tin and cut into six slices. Decorate each slice with whipped cream and the marbled chocolate caraque. Serve immediately.

mississippi mud pie

Serves 8

Difficulty: Medium

Prep: 35 mins, plus chilling and cooling
Cook: 1 hour 10 mins

INGREDIENTS

225 g/8 oz plain flour, plus
  extra for dusting

2 tbsp cocoa powder

140 g/5 oz butter

2 tbsp caster sugar

1–2 tbsp cold water

425 ml/15 fl oz whipped
  double cream and milk
  chocolate flakes, to
  decorate

FILLING

175 g/6 oz butter

350 g/12 oz soft dark
  brown sugar

4 eggs, lightly beaten

4 tbsp cocoa powder, sifted

150 g/5½ oz plain chocolate,
  melted

300 ml/10 fl oz single cream

1 tsp chocolate extract

STEP 1. Sift the flour and cocoa powder into a mixing bowl. Rub in the butter with your fingertips until the mixture resembles fine breadcrumbs. Stir in the caster sugar and enough cold water to mix to a soft dough. Wrap the dough in clingfilm and chill in the refrigerator for 15 minutes.

STEP 2. Preheat the oven to 190°C/375°F/Gas Mark 5. Roll out the dough on a lightly floured work surface and use to line a 23-cm/9-inch loose-based flan tin or ceramic flan dish. Line with baking paper and fill with baking beans. Bake in the preheated oven for 15 minutes. Remove the paper and beans and cook for a further 10 minutes until crisp.

STEP 3. To make the filling, put the butter and brown sugar into a mixing bowl and cream together, then gradually beat in the eggs with the cocoa powder. Beat the melted chocolate into the mixture, then beat in the single cream and chocolate extract.

STEP 4. Reduce the oven temperature to 160°C/325°F/Gas Mark 3. Pour the mixture into the pastry case and bake for 45 minutes, or until the filling has set gently.

STEP 5. Leave to cool completely, then transfer to a serving plate. Cover with the whipped cream. Decorate the pie with chocolate flakes and chill until ready to serve.

blackberry flan

Serves 6

Difficulty: Medium

Prep: 30 mins, plus 1 hour chilling, and cooling
Cook: 20 mins

INGREDIENTS

140 g/5 oz plain flour, plus
  extra for dusting

25 g/1 oz cocoa powder

55 g/2 oz icing sugar

pinch of salt

85 g/3 oz butter, cut into
  small pieces

½ egg yolk

FILLING

300 ml/10 fl oz double cream

175 g/6 oz blackberry jam

225 g/8 oz plain chocolate,
  broken into pieces

25 g/1 oz butter, cut into
  small pieces

SAUCE

675 g/1 lb 8 oz blackberries,
  plus extra to decorate

1 tbsp lemon juice

2 tbsp caster sugar

2 tbsp crème de cassis

STEP 1. Sift the flour, cocoa powder, icing sugar and salt into a mixing bowl and make a well in the centre. Put the butter and egg yolk into the well and gradually mix in the dry ingredients. Lightly knead, then shape into a ball. Wrap the dough in clingfilm and chill in the refrigerator for 1 hour.

STEP 2. Preheat the oven to 180°C/350°F/Gas Mark 4. Roll out the dough on a lightly floured work surface and use to line a 30 x 10-cm/12 x 4-inch rectangular flan tin. Prick with a fork, line the base with baking paper and fill with baking beans. Bake in the preheated oven for 15 minutes. Remove the paper and beans. Set aside to cool.

STEP 3. To make the filling, put the cream and jam into a saucepan and bring to the boil over a low heat. Remove from the heat, stir in the chocolate and then the butter until melted and smooth. Pour the mixture into the pastry case and set aside to cool.

STEP 4. To make the sauce, put the blackberries, lemon juice and caster sugar into a food processor and process until smooth. Strain through a nylon sieve into a bowl and stir in the crème de cassis. Set aside.

STEP 5. Remove the flan from the tin and place on a serving plate. Arrange the remaining blackberries on top and brush with a little of the sauce. Serve the flan with the remaining sauce on the side.

chocolate & raspberry pavlova

Serves 6

Difficulty: Medium

Prep: 30 mins, plus cooling and chilling
Cook: 1 hour

INGREDIENTS

MERINGUE

4 egg whites

225 g/8 oz caster sugar

1 tsp cornflour

1 tsp white wine vinegar

1 tsp vanilla extract

TOPPING

300 ml/10 fl oz double cream

1 tbsp caster sugar

2 tbsp framboise liqueur

175 g/6 oz fresh raspberries

55 g/2 oz plain
  chocolate shavings

STEP 1. Preheat the oven to 150°C/300°F/Gas Mark 2.

STEP 2. To make the meringue, put the egg whites into a clean, greasefree bowl and whisk until stiff peaks hold. Gradually whisk in 115 g/4 oz of the sugar. Put the remaining sugar and the cornflour into a separate bowl, mix to combine, then whisk into the egg white mixture; it should be very shiny and firm. Quickly fold in the vinegar and vanilla extract.

STEP 3. Draw a 25-cm/10-inch circle on a sheet of baking paper, turn the paper over and place it on a baking tray. Pile the meringue onto the paper and spread evenly to the edge of the circle; swirl it around on top to make an attractive shape. Bake in the centre of the preheated oven for 1 hour.

STEP 4. Remove from the oven, leave to cool slightly, then peel off the paper. Place the meringue on a large serving plate. It will shrink and crack but do not worry about this.

STEP 5. Make the topping 1 hour before serving. Put the cream, sugar and liqueur into a bowl and whip until thick and floppy. Pile on top of the meringue and scatter over the raspberries and chocolate shavings. Chill until ready to serve.

chocolate mousse tart

Serves 8

Difficulty: Easy

Prep: 25 mins, plus cooling and 8 hours chilling
Cook: 5 mins

INGREDIENTS

85 g/3 oz digestive biscuits,
  crushed

85 g/3 oz amaretti biscuits,
  crushed

70 g/2½ oz butter, melted

FILLING

200 g/7 oz plain chocolate,
  broken into pieces

115 g/4 oz milk chocolate,
  broken into pieces

3 eggs, separated

55 g/2 oz caster sugar

chocolate flakes,
  to decorate

STEP 1. Put the digestive biscuits and amaretti biscuits into a bowl with the butter and mix well together. Press well into the base of a 23-cm/9-inch springform cake tin. Chill in the refrigerator.

STEP 2. Meanwhile, to make the filling, put the plain chocolate and milk chocolate into a heatproof bowl set over a saucepan of gently simmering water and heat until melted. Leave to cool slightly, then add the egg yolks and mix well.

STEP 3. Put the egg whites into a clean, greasefree bowl and whisk until soft peaks hold, then add the sugar and whisk until stiff.

STEP 4. Fold the chocolate into the egg whites and pour over the biscuit base. Chill in the refrigerator for 8 hours, or overnight.

STEP 5. When you are ready to serve the tart, unclip and remove the springform, transfer the tart to a serving dish and crumble the chocolate flakes over the top.

brownie bottom cheesecake

Serves 12

Difficulty: Medium

Prep: 30 mins, plus cooling and 4 hours chilling
Cook: 1 hour 15 mins–1 hour 25 mins

INGREDIENTS

115 g/4 oz butter, plus extra
  for greasing

115 g/4 oz plain chocolate

200 g/7 oz caster sugar

2 eggs, beaten

50 ml /2 fl oz milk

115 g/4 oz plain flour, plus
  extra for dusting

FILLING

500 g/1 lb 2 oz soft cheese

125 g/4½ oz caster sugar

3 eggs, beaten

1 tsp vanilla extract

125 ml/4 fl oz natural yogurt

melted plain chocolate,
  for drizzling

STEP 1. Preheat the oven to 180°C/350°F/Gas Mark 4. Lightly grease a 23-cm/9-inch square baking tin and dust with flour, shaking out the excess.

STEP 2. Put the butter and chocolate into a heatproof bowl set over a saucepan of gently simmering water and heat, stirring frequently, until smooth. Remove the bowl from the pan and beat in the sugar.

STEP 3. Add the eggs and milk, beating well. Stir in the flour, mixing until just blended. Spoon into the prepared tin, spreading evenly.

STEP 4. Bake in the preheated oven for 25 minutes. Remove from the oven and reduce the oven temperature to 160°C/325°F/Gas Mark 3.

STEP 5. To make the filling, put the cheese, sugar, eggs and vanilla extract into a bowl and beat together until well blended. Stir in the yogurt, then pour the mixture over the brownie base. Bake for a further 45–55 minutes, or until the centre is almost set.

STEP 6. Run a knife around the edge of the cake to loosen from the tin. Leave in the tin to cool completely. Chill in the refrigerator for 4 hours or overnight before cutting into slices. Serve drizzled with melted chocolate.

deep chocolate cheesecake

Serves 6–8

Difficulty: Easy

Prep: 25 mins, plus 4 hours chilling
Cook: None

INGREDIENTS

115 g/4 oz digestive biscuits, crushed

2 tsp cocoa powder

55 g/2 oz butter, melted, plus extra for greasing

FILLING

800 g/1 lb 12 oz mascarpone cheese

200 g/7 oz icing sugar, sifted

juice of ½ orange

finely grated rind of 1 orange

175 g/6 oz plain chocolate, melted

2 tbsp brandy

plain chocolate leaves, to decorate

STEP 1. Grease a 20-cm/8-inch loose-based round cake tin.

STEP 2. Put the biscuits, cocoa powder and melted butter into a mixing bowl and mix well together. Press the mixture evenly over the base of the prepared tin.

STEP 3. To make the filling, put the mascarpone cheese and icing sugar into a separate mixing bowl and stir in the orange juice and orange rind. Add the chocolate and brandy and mix together until thoroughly combined. Spread the mixture evenly over the biscuit layer. Cover with clingfilm and chill in the refrigerator for at least 4 hours.

STEP 4. Remove the cheesecake from the refrigerator, turn out onto a serving platter and decorate with chocolate leaves. Serve immediately.

*Note: This cheesecake will keep well in the fridge for up to 5 days. However, don't attempt to freeze it – only baked cheesecakes are suitable for freezing.

white chocolate cheesecake

Serves 8

Difficulty: Medium

Prep: 30 mins, plus cooling

Cook: 1 hour 10 mins

INGREDIENTS

55 g/2 oz butter

200 g/7 oz digestive biscuits, crushed

85 g/3 oz chopped walnuts

FILLING

450 g/1 lb mascarpone cheese

2 eggs, beaten

3 tbsp caster sugar

250 g/9 oz white chocolate, broken into pieces

300 g/10½ oz strawberries, hulled and quartered

TOPPING

175 g/6 oz mascarpone cheese

50 g/1¾ oz white chocolate shavings

4 strawberries, halved

STEP 1. Preheat the oven to 150°C/300°F/Gas Mark 2. Put the butter into a saucepan over a low heat and heat until melted, then stir in the crushed biscuits and nuts. Spoon into a 23-cm/9-inch round springform cake tin and press evenly over the base with the back of a spoon. Set aside.

STEP 2. To make the filling, put the mascarpone cheese into a bowl and beat until smooth, then beat in the eggs and sugar. Put the chocolate into a heatproof bowl set over a saucepan of gently simmering water and stir until smooth. Remove from the heat and leave to cool slightly, then stir into the cheese mixture. Stir in the strawberries.

STEP 3. Spoon the mixture into the tin, spread out evenly and smooth the surface. Bake in the preheated oven for 1 hour, or until the filling is just firm. Switch off the oven, open the door slightly and leave the cheesecake inside until completely cold. Transfer to a serving plate.

STEP 4. To make the topping, spread the mascarpone cheese on top of the cheesecake. Decorate with the chocolate shavings and the strawberry halves.

small bites & drinks

chocolate truffles

Makes 40–50

Difficulty: Medium

Prep: 15 mins, plus chilling
Cook: 5 mins

INGREDIENTS

350 g/12 oz plain chocolate,
  broken into pieces

115 g/4 oz butter

400 ml/14 fl oz double cream

1 tbsp vanilla extract

grated coconut, cocoa
  powder, sifted icing sugar
  and chopped nuts,
  for coating

STEP 1. Line a baking tray with baking paper. Put the chocolate, butter and cream into a heatproof bowl set over a saucepan of gently simmering water and stir until melted and combined. Stir in the vanilla extract, mix well and pour into a shallow dish. Chill in the refrigerator until firm enough to roll into balls.

STEP 2. Working quickly, use a melon baller to scoop small balls out of the chilled chocolate mixture.

STEP 3. Spread out the grated coconut, cocoa powder, icing sugar and chopped nuts on separate plates and roll the chocolate balls in the various coatings.

STEP 4. Place the coated balls on the prepared tray, cover and chill until ready to serve.

italian chocolate truffles

Makes 24

Difficulty: Easy

Prep: 20 mins, plus chilling
Cook: 5 mins

INGREDIENTS

175 g/6 oz plain chocolate,
  broken into pieces

2 tbsp amaretto or orange
  liqueur

3 tbsp butter

4 tbsp icing sugar

50 g/1¾ oz ground almonds

50 g/1¾ oz milk chocolate,
  grated

STEP 1. Put the plain chocolate and the amaretto into a heatproof bowl set over a saucepan of gently simmering water and stir until the chocolate is melted and well combined with the liqueur.

STEP 2. Add the butter and stir until melted. Stir in the icing sugar and the ground almonds.

STEP 3. Chill the mixture until firm enough to roll into balls. Use a melon baller to scoop 24 balls out of the cooled mixture.

STEP 4. Place the grated chocolate on a plate and roll the balls in the chocolate until coated.

STEP 5. Put the truffles into paper cases and chill until ready to serve.

*Note: The chilled mixture will begin to soften as soon as you take it out of the fridge, so you will need to work very quickly when rolling the truffles.

white chocolate truffles

Makes 20

Difficulty: Medium

Prep: 20 mins, plus 2½ hours chilling, and setting
Cook: 10 mins

INGREDIENTS

2 tbsp butter

5 tbsp double cream

225 g/8 oz Swiss white chocolate, broken into pieces

1 tbsp orange liqueur (optional)

100 g/3½ oz white chocolate, broken into pieces, for coating

STEP 1. Line a Swiss roll tin with baking paper.

STEP 2. Put the butter and cream into a small saucepan and bring slowly to the boil, stirring constantly. Boil for 1 minute, then remove from the heat.

STEP 3. Add the chocolate to the cream. Stir until melted, then beat in the liqueur, if using.

STEP 4. Pour the mixture into the prepared tin and chill for about 2 hours until firm enough to roll into balls. Working quickly, use a melon baller to scoop 20 balls out of the chilled mixture, then chill the balls for 30 minutes.

STEP 5. Put the white chocolate into a heatproof bowl set over a saucepan of gently simmering water and heat until melted. Dip the balls in the chocolate, allowing the excess to drip back into the bowl. Place on a sheet of non-stick baking paper, swirl the chocolate with the tines of a fork and leave to set.

nutty chocolate clusters

Makes 30

Difficulty: Easy

Prep: 20 mins, plus chilling and cooling
Cook: 10 mins

INGREDIENTS

175 g/6 oz white chocolate,
  broken into pieces

100 g/3½ oz digestive
  biscuits

100 g/3½ oz macadamia nuts
  or Brazil nuts, chopped

25 g/1 oz stem ginger,
  chopped (optional)

175 g/6 oz plain chocolate,
  broken into pieces

STEP 1. Line a baking tray with baking paper. Put the white chocolate into a large heatproof bowl set over a saucepan of gently simmering water and stir until melted.

STEP 2. Break the digestive biscuits into small pieces. Stir the crumbs into the melted chocolate with the chopped nuts and the ginger, if using.

STEP 3. Place 30 heaped teaspoons of the mixture on the prepared baking tray. Chill in the refrigerator until set, then remove from the baking paper.

STEP 4. Put the plain chocolate into a large heatproof bowl set over a saucepan of gently simmering water and heat until melted. Leave to cool slightly. Dip the clusters into the melted chocolate, allowing the excess to drip back into the bowl. Return the clusters to the baking tray and chill in the refrigerator until set.

chocolate marshmallow fudge

Makes 35–40 pieces

Difficulty: Easy

Prep: 15 mins, plus chilling and setting

Cook: 10 mins

INGREDIENTS

115 g/4 oz plain chocolate, broken into pieces

200 g/7 oz white mini marshmallows

70 g/2½ oz butter, plus extra for greasing

2 tsp water

115 g/4 oz blanched almonds, roughly chopped

STEP 1. Lightly grease a 20-cm/8-inch square cake tin.

STEP 2. Put the chocolate into a heatproof bowl set over a saucepan of gently simmering water and heat until melted. Put the marshmallows, butter and water into a large, heavy-based saucepan over a low heat and heat, stirring frequently, until melted.

STEP 3. Remove from the heat and pour the chocolate into the marshmallow mixture. Add the almonds and stir until well mixed.

STEP 4. Pour the mixture into the prepared tin and chill until firm. Turn out onto a chopping board and cut into squares. Chill until required.

rich chocolate fudge

Makes about 50

Difficulty: Easy

Prep: 10 mins, plus chilling
Cook: 15–20 mins

INGREDIENTS

PIECES

85 g/3 oz butter, plus extra
  for greasing

450 g/1 lb sugar

150 ml/5 fl oz evaporated
  milk

150 g/5½ oz plain chocolate,
  broken into pieces

2 tbsp cocoa powder

STEP 1. Grease an 18-cm/7-inch square cake tin and line with baking paper. Put all the ingredients into a large saucepan over a low heat and heat, stirring, until the sugar dissolves and the chocolate has melted.

STEP 2. Bring to the boil and boil for 10–15 minutes, stirring occasionally. Pour into the prepared tin and smooth the top. Chill in the refrigerator until firm.

STEP 3. Turn out the fudge onto a chopping board and cut into squares. Chill until required.

*Note: Fudge lends itself to being combined with other ingredients, such as juicy raisins or chopped nuts – chopped pistachio nuts are a good choice for the colour contrast. Just stir them into the fudge mixture before pouring into the cake tin.

brazil nut brittle

Makes 20

Difficulty: Easy

Prep: 15 mins, plus setting
Cook: 10 mins

INGREDIENTS

sunflower oil, for oiling

350 g/12 oz plain chocolate,
  broken into pieces

100 g/3½ oz shelled Brazil
  nuts, chopped

175 g/6 oz white chocolate,
  roughly chopped

175 g/6 oz fudge,
  roughly chopped

STEP 1. Oil the base of a 20-cm/8-inch square cake tin and line with baking paper. Put half the plain chocolate into a heatproof bowl set over a saucepan of gently simmering water and heat until melted, then spread evenly in the prepared tin.

STEP 2. Sprinkle with the chopped nuts, white chocolate and fudge. Put the remaining plain chocolate into a heatproof bowl set over a saucepan of gently simmering water and heat until melted, then pour over the top.

STEP 3. Leave the brittle to set, then break up into jagged pieces using the tip of a strong knife.

*Note: Chocolate nut brittle is both easy to make and very impressive. Use any nuts you like, or a combination of several kinds, and vary the chocolate according to taste. The secret to a good chocolate brittle is to use only the best quality chocolate.

chocolate cherries

Makes 24

Difficulty: Medium

Prep: 30 mins, plus chilling and setting
Cook: 10 mins

INGREDIENTS

12 glacé cherries

2 tbsp dark rum or brandy

250 g/9 oz marzipan

125 g/4½ oz plain chocolate,
  broken into pieces

milk chocolate, plain
  chocolate or white
  chocolate, to decorate

STEP 1. Line a baking tray with a sheet of baking paper.

STEP 2. Cut the cherries in half and put into a small bowl. Add the rum and stir to coat. Leave the cherries to soak for at least 1 hour, stirring occasionally.

STEP 3. Divide the marzipan into 24 pieces and roll each piece into a ball. Press half a cherry into the top of each marzipan ball.

STEP 4. Put the chocolate into a heatproof bowl set over a saucepan of gently simmering water and heat until melted.

STEP 5. Dip each marzipan ball into the melted chocolate using a cocktail stick, allowing the excess to drip back into the bowl. Place the coated cherries on the prepared tray and chill in the refrigerator until set.

STEP 6. To decorate, put a little chocolate into a heatproof bowl set over a saucepan of gently simmering water and heat until melted. Drizzle it over the top of the coated cherries and leave to set.

chocolate creams

Makes about 30

Difficulty: Medium

Prep: 25 mins, plus setting
Cook: 10 mins

INGREDIENTS

200 g/7 oz plain chocolate,
  broken into pieces

2 tbsp single cream

225 g/8 oz icing sugar

cocoa powder, for dusting

STEP 1. Line a baking tray with baking paper. Put 55 g/2 oz of the chocolate into a heatproof bowl set over a saucepan of gently simmering water and heat until melted. Stir in the cream, then remove the bowl from the pan.

STEP 2. Sift the icing sugar into the melted chocolate, then mix well together with a fork. Knead to a firm, smooth, pliable mixture.

STEP 3. Turn out onto a work surface lightly dusted with cocoa powder and roll out to a thickness of 5-mm/¼-inch, then cut into rounds with a 2.5-cm/1-inch plain cutter.

STEP 4. Transfer to the prepared tray and leave to stand for about 12 hours, or overnight, until set and dry.

STEP 5. Line a baking tray with baking paper. Put the remaining chocolate into a heatproof bowl set over a saucepan of gently simmering water and heat until melted. Using two forks, carefully dip each chocolate cream into the melted chocolate. Lift it out quickly, allowing any excess chocolate to drain against the side of the bowl, and place on the prepared tray. Leave to set.

mini florentines

Makes 20–30

Difficulty: Hard

Prep: 30 mins, plus cooling and setting
Cook: 25–30 mins

INGREDIENTS

75 g/2¾ oz butter

75 g/2¾ oz caster sugar

25 g/1 oz sultanas or raisins

25 g/1 oz glacé cherries,
  chopped

25 g/1 oz crystallized stem
  ginger, finely chopped

25 g/1 oz sunflower seeds

100 g/3½ oz flaked almonds

2 tbsp double cream

175 g/6 oz plain or
  milk chocolate,
  broken into pieces

STEP 1. Preheat the oven to 180°C/350°F/Gas Mark 4. Line two baking trays with baking paper. Put the butter into a small saucepan over a low heat and heat until melted. Add the sugar, stir until dissolved, then bring to the boil. Remove from the heat and stir in the sultanas, glacé cherries, ginger, sunflower seeds and almonds. Mix well, then beat in the cream.

STEP 2. Place small, well-spaced teaspoons of mixture on the prepared trays. Bake in the preheated oven for 10–12 minutes, or until light golden. Remove from the oven and, while still hot, use a round cutter to pull in the edges to form perfect circles. Leave to cool and become crisp before removing from the trays.

STEP 3. Put the chocolate into a heatproof bowl set over a saucepan of gently simmering water and heat until melted. Spread most of the chocolate on a sheet of baking paper. When it is on the point of setting, place the biscuits flat side down on the chocolate and leave them until the chocolate is completely hard.

STEP 4. Cut around the florentines and remove from the baking paper. Spread the remaining chocolate on the coated side of the florentines, using a fork to mark waves. Leave to set.

chocolate pistachio biscotti

Makes 24

Difficulty: Easy

Prep: 30 mins, plus cooling
Cook: 35 mins

INGREDIENTS

25 g/1 oz butter, plus extra
  for greasing

175 g/6 oz plain chocolate,
  broken into pieces

350 g/12 oz self-raising flour,
  plus extra for dusting

1½ tsp baking powder

85 g/3 oz caster sugar

70 g/2½ oz polenta

finely grated rind of
  1 lemon

2 tsp amaretto

1 egg, beaten

115 g/4 oz pistachio nuts,
  roughly chopped

sifted icing sugar, for dusting

STEP 1. Preheat the oven to 160°C/325°F/Gas Mark 3. Grease a baking tray.

STEP 2. Put the butter and chocolate into a heatproof bowl set over a saucepan of gently simmering water and stir until melted and smooth. Remove from the heat and leave to cool slightly.

STEP 3. Sift the flour and baking powder into a mixing bowl and mix in the caster sugar, polenta, lemon rind, amaretto, egg and pistachio nuts. Stir in the chocolate mixture and mix to a soft dough.

STEP 4. Lightly dust your hands with flour, divide the dough in half and shape each piece into a 28-cm/11-inch long cylinder. Transfer the cylinders to the prepared tray and flatten with the palm of your hand to a thickness of about 2 cm/¾ inch. Bake in the preheated oven for about 20 minutes until firm to the touch. Remove from the oven but do not switch off the oven.

STEP 5. Leave the cylinders to cool on the tray, then transfer to a chopping board and slice diagonally into thick biscuits. Return to the tray and bake for a further 10 minutes until crisp. Remove from the oven and transfer to wire racks and leave to cool completely. Lightly dust with icing sugar before serving.

chocolate liqueurs

Makes 40

Difficulty: Hard

Prep: 30 mins, plus 20 mins chilling, and setting
Cook: 5 mins

INGREDIENTS

100 g/3½ oz plain chocolate,
  broken into pieces

20 glacé cherries, or
  20 hazelnuts or
  macadamia nuts

50 g/1¾ oz plain chocolate,
  melted, and marbled
  chocolate caraque, to
  decorate

FILLING

150 ml/5 fl oz double cream

2 tbsp icing sugar

4 tbsp liqueur

STEP 1. Line a baking tray with baking paper. Put the chocolate pieces into a heatproof bowl set over a saucepan of gently simmering water and heat until melted. Spoon into 40 paper sweet cases, spreading up the sides with a spoon or brush. Place upside down on the prepared tray and leave to set.

STEP 2. Carefully peel away the paper cases. Place a cherry or nut in each cup.

STEP 3. To make the filling, put the cream into a mixing bowl and sift in the icing sugar. Whip the cream until it just holds its shape, then whisk in the liqueur.

STEP 4. Spoon the cream into a piping bag fitted with a 1-cm/½-inch plain nozzle and pipe a little into each chocolate case. Leave to chill for 20 minutes.

STEP 5. To decorate, spoon the melted chocolate over the cream to cover it. Add the caraque and leave to set.

ladies' kisses

Makes 20

Difficulty: Medium

Prep: 30 mins, plus 1½–2 hours chilling, and cooling
Cook: 25–30 mins

INGREDIENTS

175 g/6 oz butter

115 g/4 oz caster sugar

1 egg yolk

100 g/3½ oz ground almonds

175 g/6 oz plain flour

55 g/2 oz plain chocolate,
  broken into pieces

STEP 1. Line three baking sheets with baking paper. Put the butter and sugar into a mixing bowl and cream together until light and fluffy. Beat in the egg yolk, then beat in the almonds and flour. Continue beating until thoroughly mixed to a dough. Shape into a ball, wrap in clingfilm and chill in the refrigerator for 1½–2 hours.

STEP 2. Preheat the oven to 160°C/325°F/Gas Mark 3. Unwrap the dough, break off walnut-sized pieces and roll them into balls between the palms of your hands. Place the dough balls on the prepared baking sheets, spaced well apart to allow for spreading. You may need to cook them in batches. Bake in the preheated oven for 20–25 minutes until golden. Carefully transfer the biscuits to wire racks and leave to cool.

STEP 3. Put the chocolate into a heatproof bowl set over a saucepan of gently simmering water and heat until melted. Spread the melted chocolate on the flat sides of the cookies and sandwich them together in pairs. Return to the wire racks and leave to cool completely.

chocolate crispy bites

Makes 16

Difficulty: Easy

Prep: 10 mins, plus cooling and chilling
Cook: 10 mins

INGREDIENTS

WHITE LAYER

55 g/2 oz butter, plus extra
for greasing

1 tbsp golden syrup

150 g/5½ oz white chocolate,
broken into small pieces

50 g/1¾ oz toasted
rice cereal

DARK LAYER

55 g/2 oz butter

2 tbsp golden syrup

125 g/4½ oz plain chocolate,
broken into small pieces

75 g/2¾ oz toasted
rice cereal

STEP 1. Grease a 20-cm/8-inch square cake tin and line with baking paper.

STEP 2. To make the white layer, put the butter, golden syrup and white chocolate into a bowl set over a saucepan of gently simmering water and heat until melted. Remove the bowl from the pan and stir in the rice cereal until combined. Press into the prepared tin and smooth the surface.

STEP 3. To make the dark layer, put the butter, golden syrup and plain chocolate into a bowl set over a saucepan of gently simmering water and heat until melted. Remove from the heat and stir in the rice cereal. Pour over the hardened white chocolate layer and leave to cool, then chill until hardened.

STEP 4. Turn out of the tin and cut into small squares using a sharp knife.

*Note: These are an elegant take on every child's favourite party cookie. Children are not usually fond of plain chocolate, so if they're for a child's party, use milk chocolate instead.

real hot chocolate

Serves 1–2

Difficulty: Easy

Prep: 5 mins, plus standing
Cook: 10 mins

INGREDIENTS

40 g/1½ oz plain chocolate,
  broken into pieces

300 ml/10 fl oz milk

milk chocolate curls,
  to decorate

STEP 1. Put the chocolate into a large, heatproof jug. Put the milk into a heavy-based saucepan and bring to the boil. Pour about a quarter of the milk onto the chocolate and leave to stand until the chocolate has softened.

STEP 2. Whisk the milk and chocolate mixture until smooth. Bring the remaining milk to the boil again, then pour onto the chocolate, whisking constantly.

STEP 3. Pour the hot chocolate into warmed mugs or cups and decorate with chocolate curls. Serve immediately.

*Note: This indulgent and warming drink owes its origins to Spanish hot chocolate, and bears only a passing resemblance to the version made with drinking chocolate powder. Add a swirl of whipped cream on top for an extra treat.

hot chocolate float

Serves 4

Difficulty: Easy

Prep: 5 mins
Cook: 10 mins

INGREDIENTS

450 ml/16 fl oz milk

225 g/8 oz plain chocolate,
 broken into small pieces

2 tbsp caster sugar

8 scoops coconut
 ice cream

8 scoops plain chocolate
 ice cream

whipped cream,
 to decorate

STEP 1. Pour the milk into a saucepan. Add the chocolate and sugar. Stir over a low heat until the chocolate has melted, the sugar has dissolved and the mixture is smooth. Remove from the heat.

STEP 2. Put 1 scoop of coconut ice cream into each of four heatproof glasses, top with a scoop of chocolate ice cream, then repeat the layers.

STEP 3. Pour the chocolate-flavoured milk into the glasses, top with whipped cream and serve immediately.

marshmallow float

Serves 4

Difficulty: Easy

Prep: 5 mins
Cook: 10 mins

INGREDIENTS

900 ml/1½ pints milk

3 tbsp caster sugar

225 g/8 oz plain chocolate,
  finely chopped

8 marshmallows

STEP 1. Pour the milk into a saucepan and bring to just below boiling. Remove from the heat and whisk in the sugar and the chocolate.

STEP 2. Pour into warmed mugs or cups, top each with 2 marshmallows and serve immediately.

mocha cream

Serves 2

Difficulty: Easy

Prep: 10 mins
Cook: None

INGREDIENTS

200 ml/7 fl oz milk

50 ml/2 fl oz single cream

1 tbsp soft light brown sugar

2 tbsp cocoa powder

1 tbsp coffee syrup or instant
 coffee powder

6 ice cubes

whipped cream and grated
 milk chocolate, to decorate

STEP 1. Put the milk, cream and sugar into a food processor and gently process until combined.

STEP 2. Add the cocoa powder and coffee syrup and process, then add the ice cubes and process until smooth.

STEP 3. Pour into glasses. Top with whipped cream, scatter the grated chocolate over the drinks and serve.

*Note: Cafés in France and Italy often serve this cooling drink with an indulgent drizzle of hot chocolate sauce, which provides a delicious contrast to the cold drink. Try it and see!

cool minty chocolate

Serves 4

Difficulty: Easy

Prep: 10 mins

Cook: 10 mins

INGREDIENTS

600 ml/1 pint ice-cold milk

6 tbsp drinking chocolate
  powder

200 ml/7 oz single cream

1 tsp peppermint extract

6 scoops chocolate-mint ice
  cream

fresh mint sprigs,
  to decorate

STEP 1. Pour half the milk into a small saucepan and stir in the drinking chocolate powder. Heat over a low heat, stirring constantly, until just below boiling and the mixture is smooth. Remove from the heat.

STEP 2. Pour the chocolate-flavoured milk into a large chilled bowl and whisk in the remaining milk. Whisk in the cream and peppermint extract and continue to whisk until cold.

STEP 3. Pour the mixture into four glasses, top each with a scoop of ice cream, decorate with a mint sprig and serve immediately.

chocolate milkshake

Serves 2

Difficulty: Easy

Prep: 5 mins
Cook: None

INGREDIENTS

150 ml/5 fl oz milk

2 tbsp chocolate syrup

400 g/14 oz chocolate
  ice cream

grated plain chocolate,
  to decorate

STEP 1. Pour the milk and chocolate syrup into a food processor and gently process until combined.

STEP 2. Add the ice cream and process until smooth. Pour the mixture into tall glasses and scatter the grated chocolate over the shakes. Serve immediately.

*Note: This is the basic recipe for a milkshake — you can vary it endlessly by substituting the syrup and the ice cream with any flavour of your choice, adjusting the decoration to suit.

Index